BELOW THE WAVES
A Sea Life Coloring Book

Original Art by David McGonigal

Below the Waves: A Sea Life Coloring Book by David McGonigal

Part of the Calming Nature Coloring Series

Cover Design by David McGonigal

Published by Mama Moon Books

www.MamaMoonBooks.com

© 2020 David McGonigal

ISBN: 9798720174149

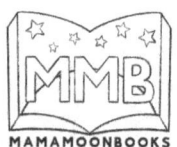

Journey below the waves with this meditative and relaxing sea life coloring book for adults, teens, and older kids. These twenty-five designs have been hand-drawn with care for stress-relief and creative expression by artist David McGonigal.

Filled with marine animals ranging from tropical coral reefs to the Pacific coast, Arctic waters to inland seas, each design is accompanied by facts about these beautiful creatures who share our earth.

If you're using markers or apply a lot of pressure with colored pencils, I suggest placing a scrap piece of paper behind the page you are coloring on to prevent bleed-through to the next design.

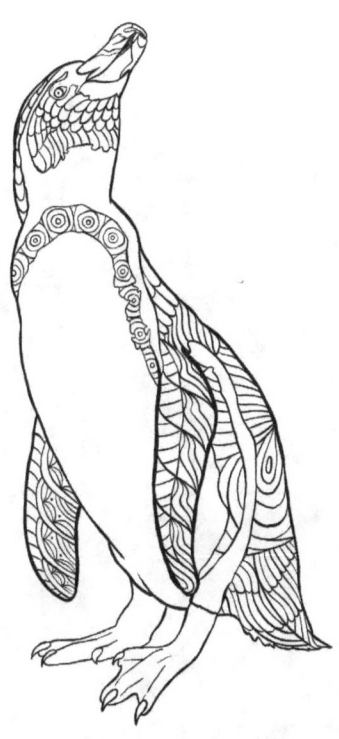

Harbor Seal
(Phoca vitulina)

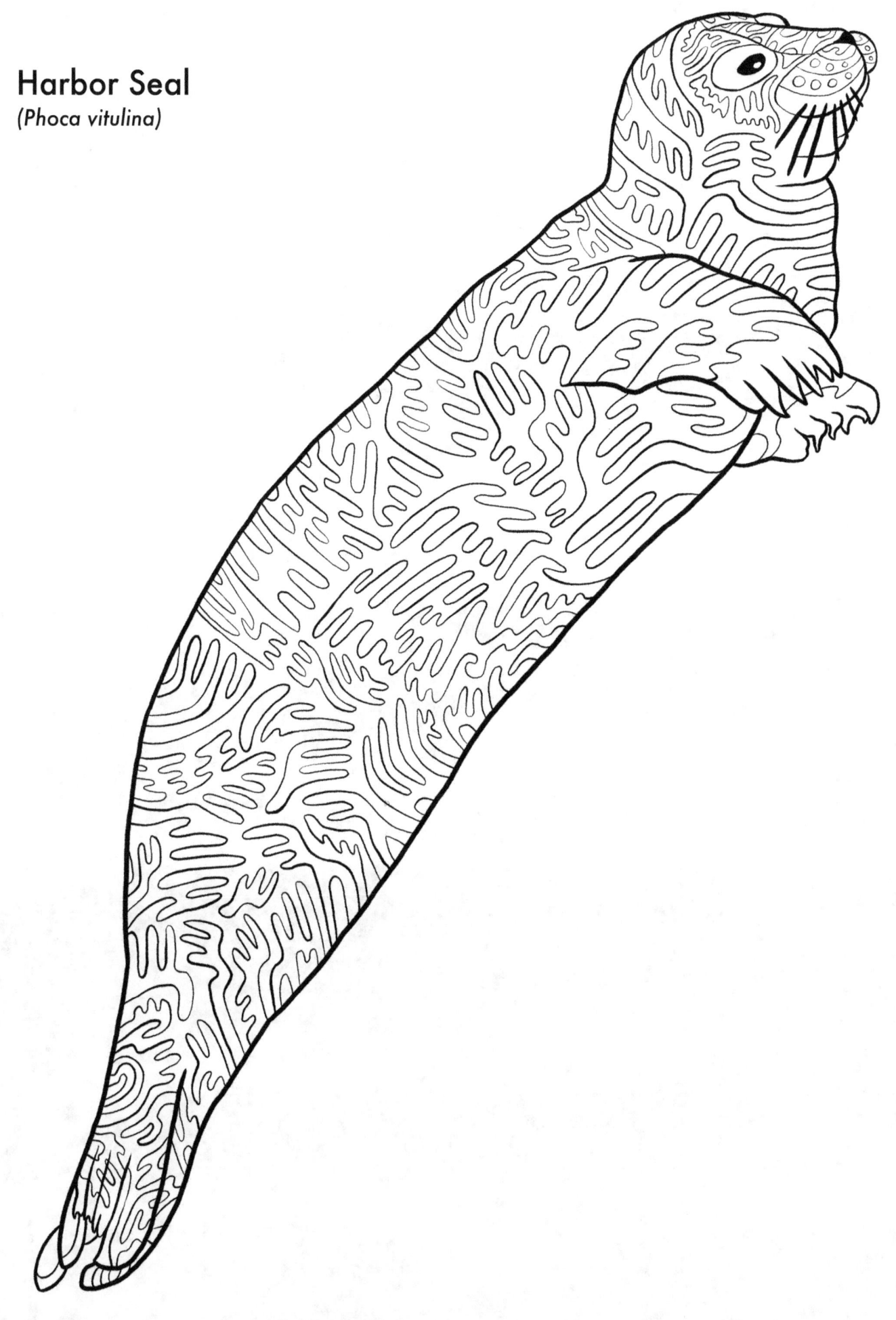

Bottlenose Dolphin
(Tursiops truncatus)

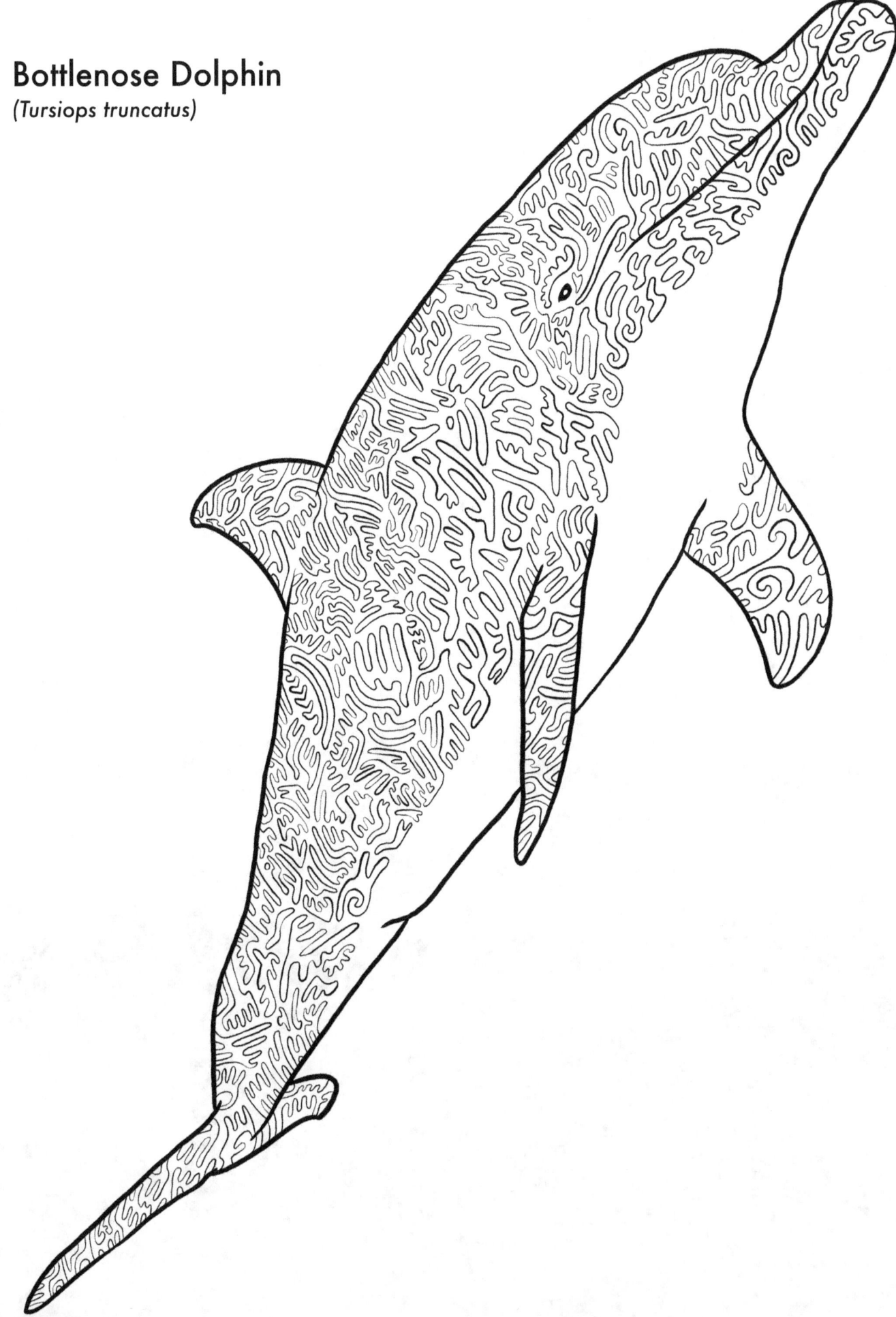

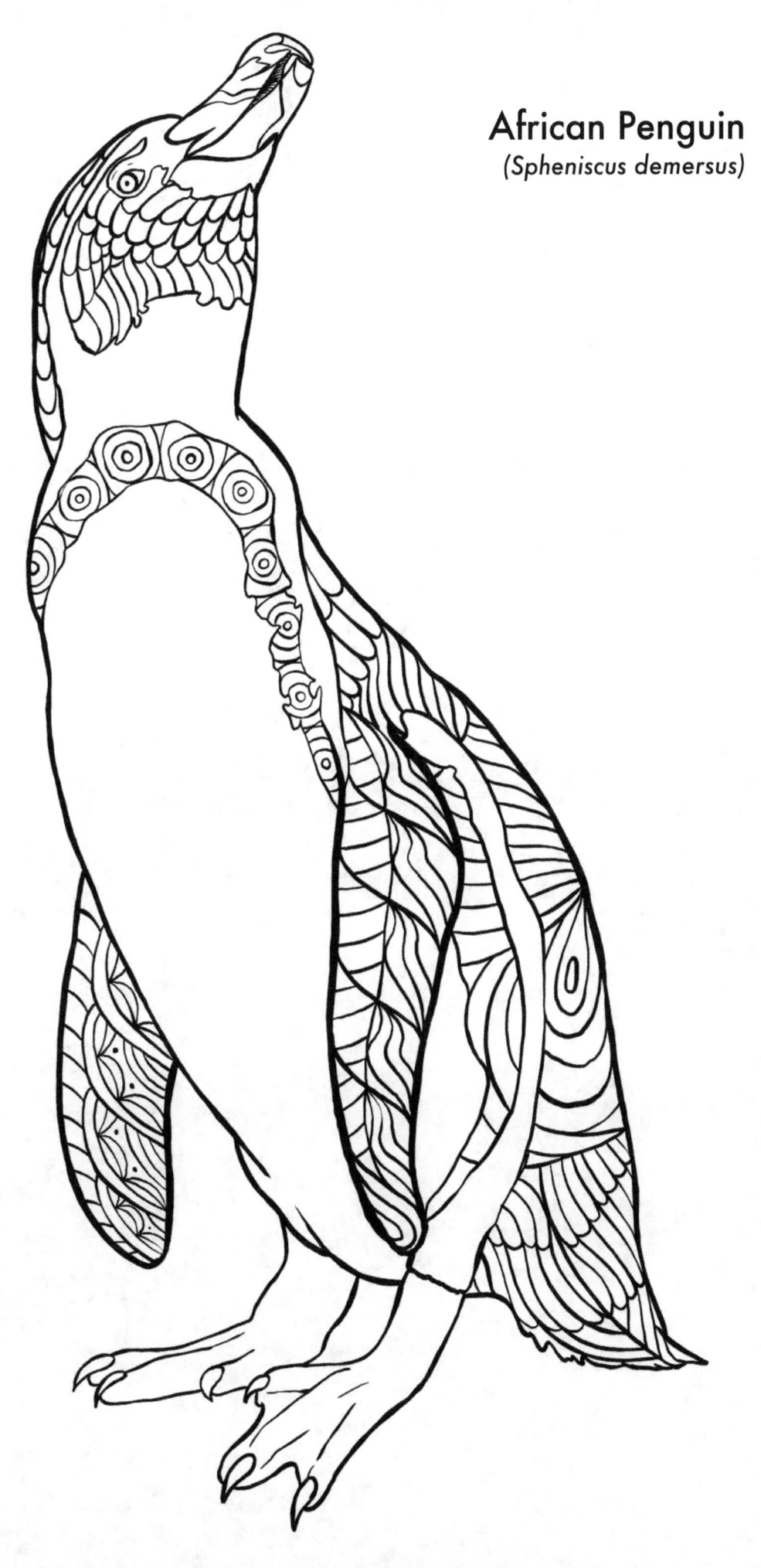

African Penguin
(Spheniscus demersus)

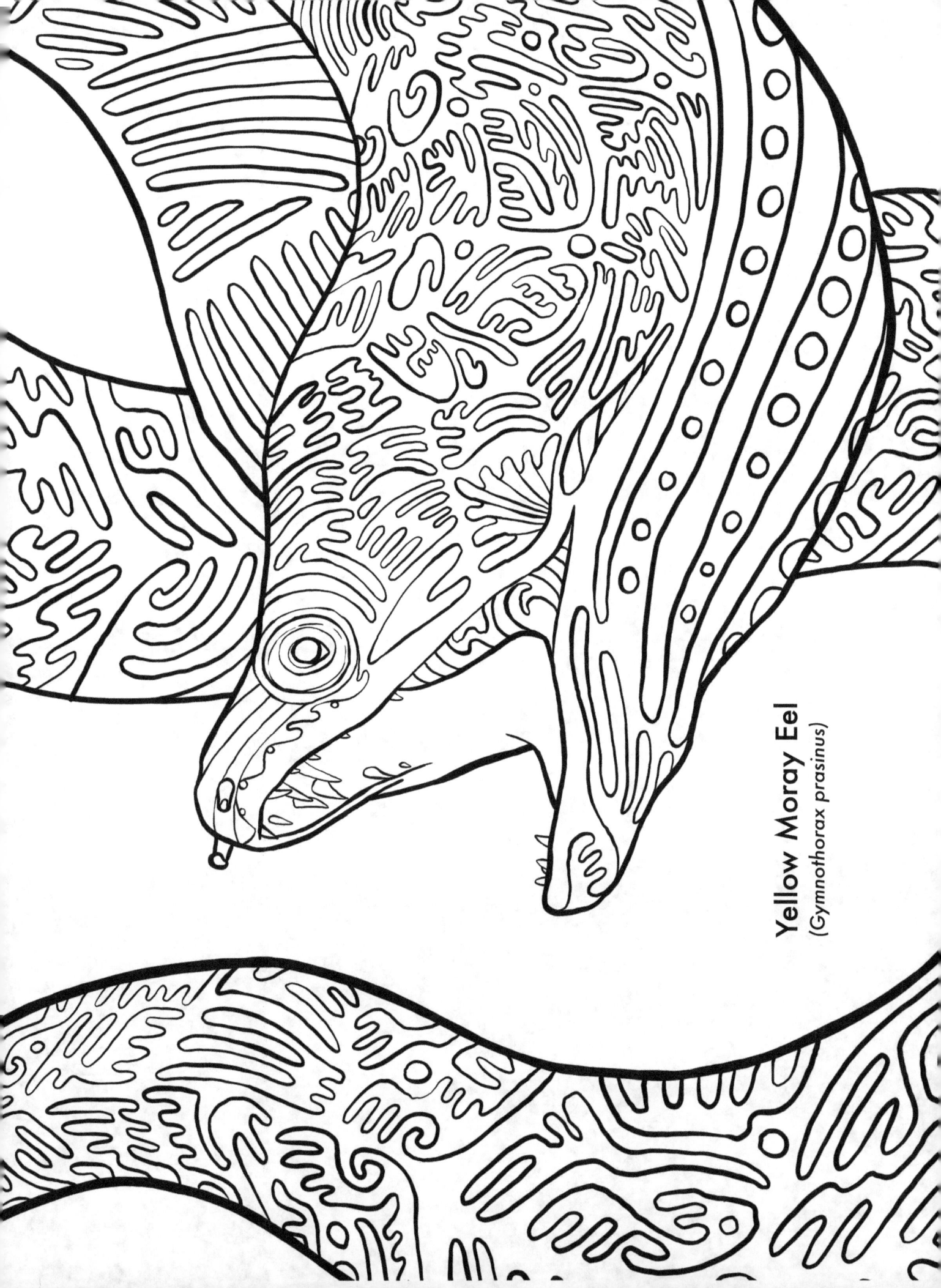

Yellow Moray Eel
(Gymnothorax prasinus)

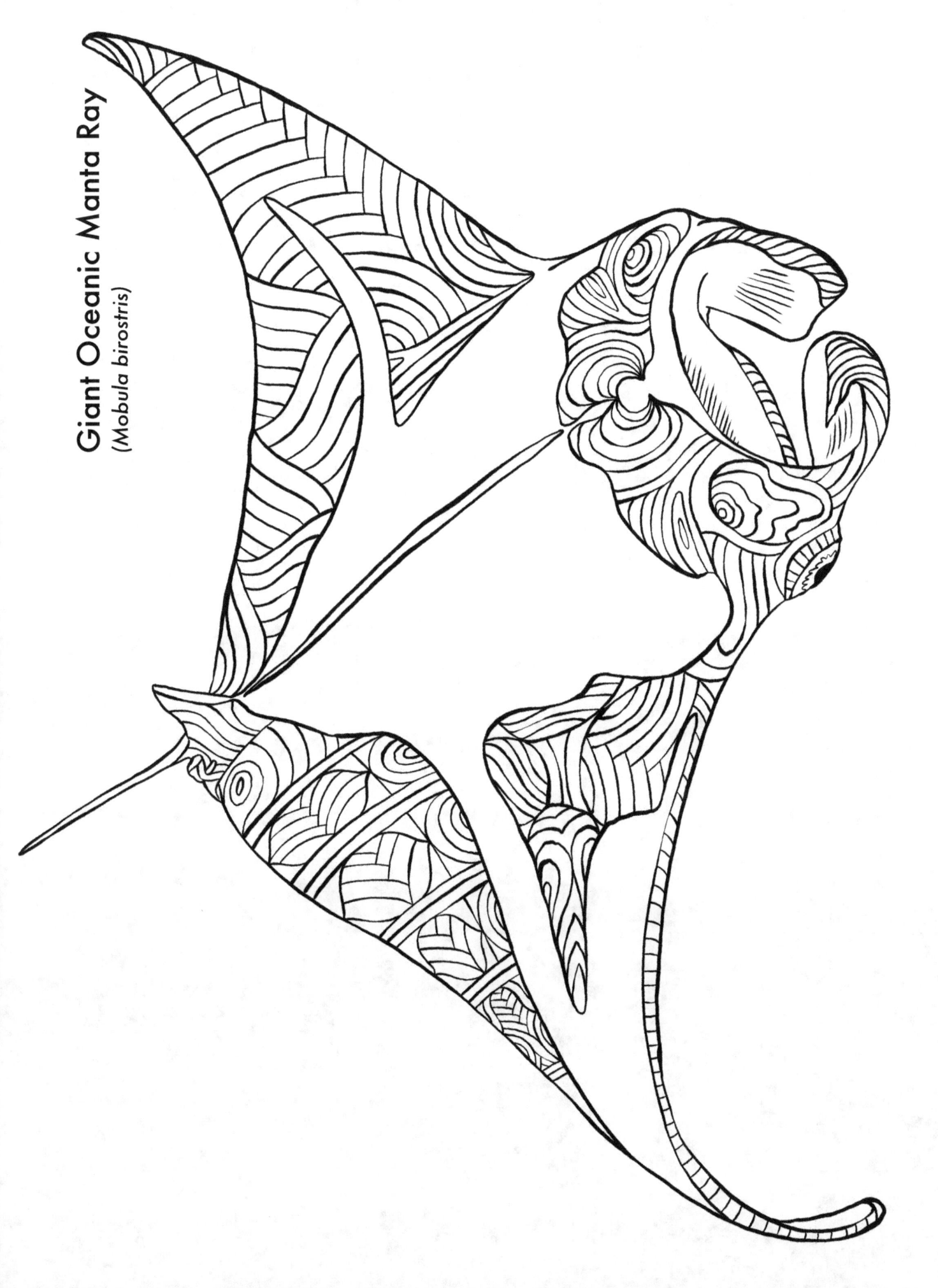

Giant Oceanic Manta Ray
(Mobula birostris)

Harbor Seal (Phoca vitulina)

The Harbor Seal lives along the Artic and temperate coastlines of the northern hemisphere, in the Pacific and Atlantic Oceans as well Baltic and North Seas. Also known as the common seal, they can reach sizes of 1.85 metres and weights of around 170 kg. They have a thick layer of blubber under their skin to help regulate body temperature when swimming and diving for food. This diet consists of fish such as mackerel, cod, salmon, and less frequently, shrimp, crabs, and squid. Harbor seals might spend several days at sea while searching for food, but will return to familiar spots on the coast to rest, usually rocky coasts to sandy beaches.

Bottlenose Dolphin (Tursiops truncates)

The range of the Bottlenose Dolphin extends all around the world, both in temperate and tropical waters. These are very social animals, living in pods which usually number 15 animals. As highly intelligent creatures, bottlenose dolphins are adept at problem-solving, and communicate through both body language and sound. This includes squeaks and whistles from the blow hole as well as vocal clicks and chatters. Through echolocation, these clicks are used when hunting to find prey. Bottlenose dolphins can reach up to 4 metres in size and up to 650 kg in weight.

African Penguin (Spheniscus demersus)

The African Penguin lives only on the south-western coast of Africa, mostly in South Africa and Namibia. Several colonies have been established on islands and the mainland, from which they swim up to 20km out to search for anchovies, sardines, as well as smaller crustaceans and squid. They are generally between 60-70 cm in size and 2.2-3.5 kg in weight. Though the population once numbered more than 4 million, human activities such as hunting and the oil industry have decimated the population to under 50,000.

Yellow Moray Eel (Gymnothorax prasinus)

The Yellow Moray Eel is found in southern Australia and New Zealand, often in and around coral reefs. They are a medium sized eel, usually reaching sizes of 75 cm. Though not generally threatening, moray eels have two sets of jaws, one for attacking and gripping prey while an inner pharyngeal jaw jumps out to pull the prey into the throat. They also produce a slimy mucous to coat their bodies which contains toxins. Moray eels are nocturnal, and during the day hide in holes and crevices throughout coral reefs.

Giant Oceanic Manta Ray (Mobula birostris)

The Giant Oceanic Manta ray is the largest ray in the world, growing up to 7 metres across and 3000 kg in weight. Though they generally stay in tropical waters, they have been found in more temperate regions. These rays travel alone and in groups, both with other rays as well as other fish, birds, and marine mammals. They subsist on zooplankton through filter feeding, as well as mesopelagic (deep-water) feeding which includes fish. When close to coastal regions, these creatures visit coral reef cleaning stations, where cleaner fish such as the cleaner wrasse travel over their body to consume parasites and loose bits of skin.

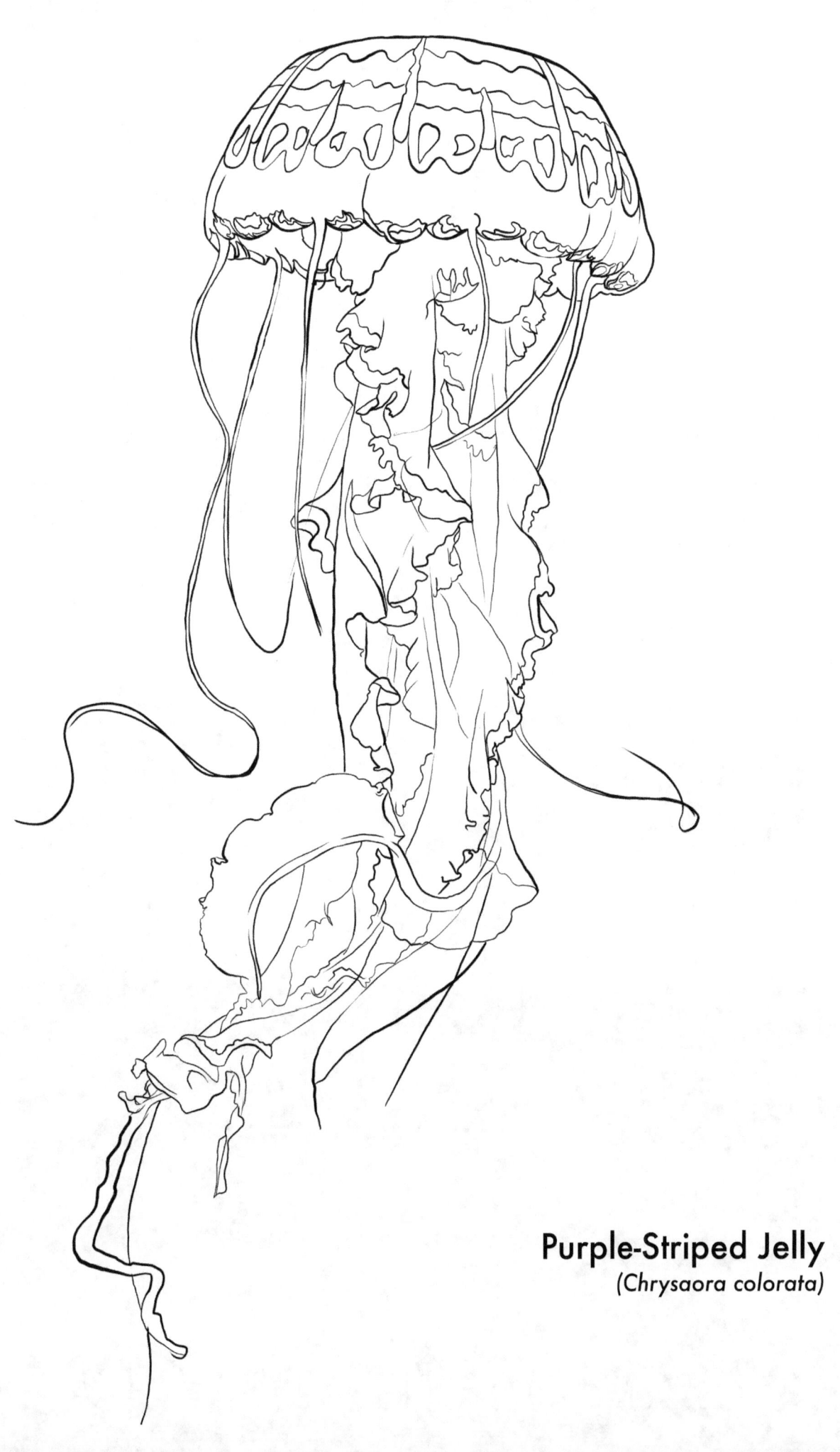

Purple-Striped Jelly
(Chrysaora colorata)

Bluelined Angelfish
(*Chaetodontoplus septentrionalis*)

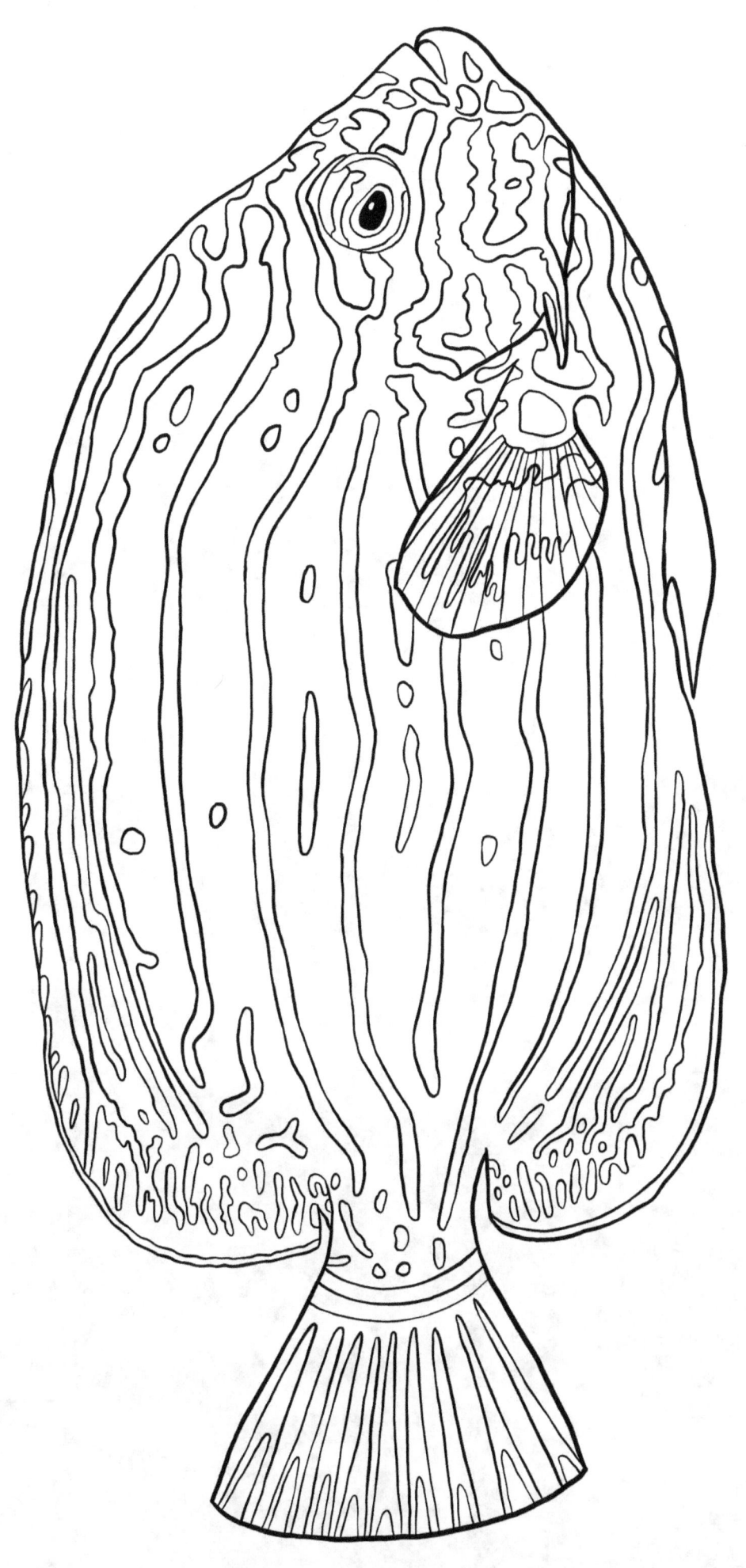

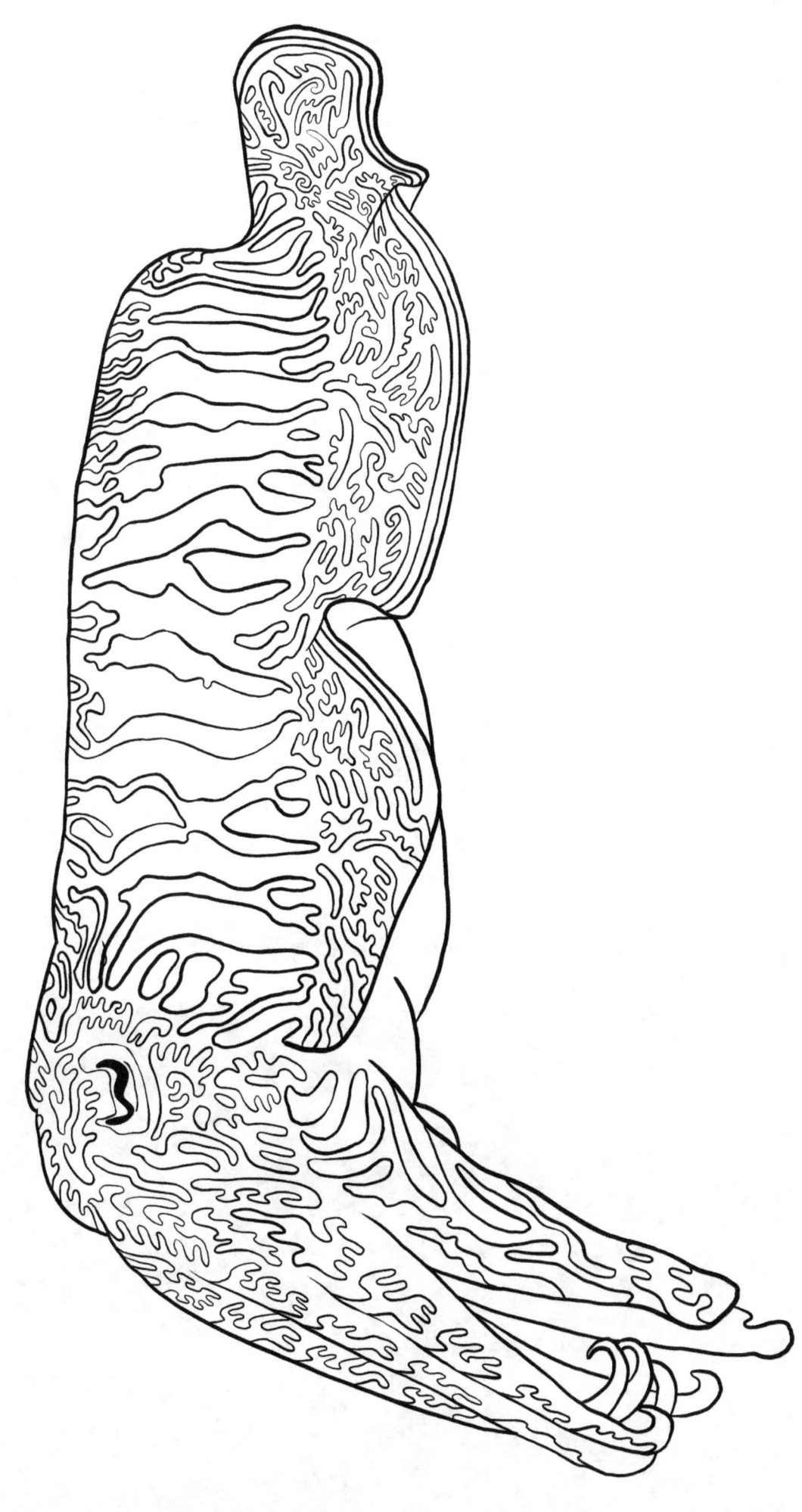

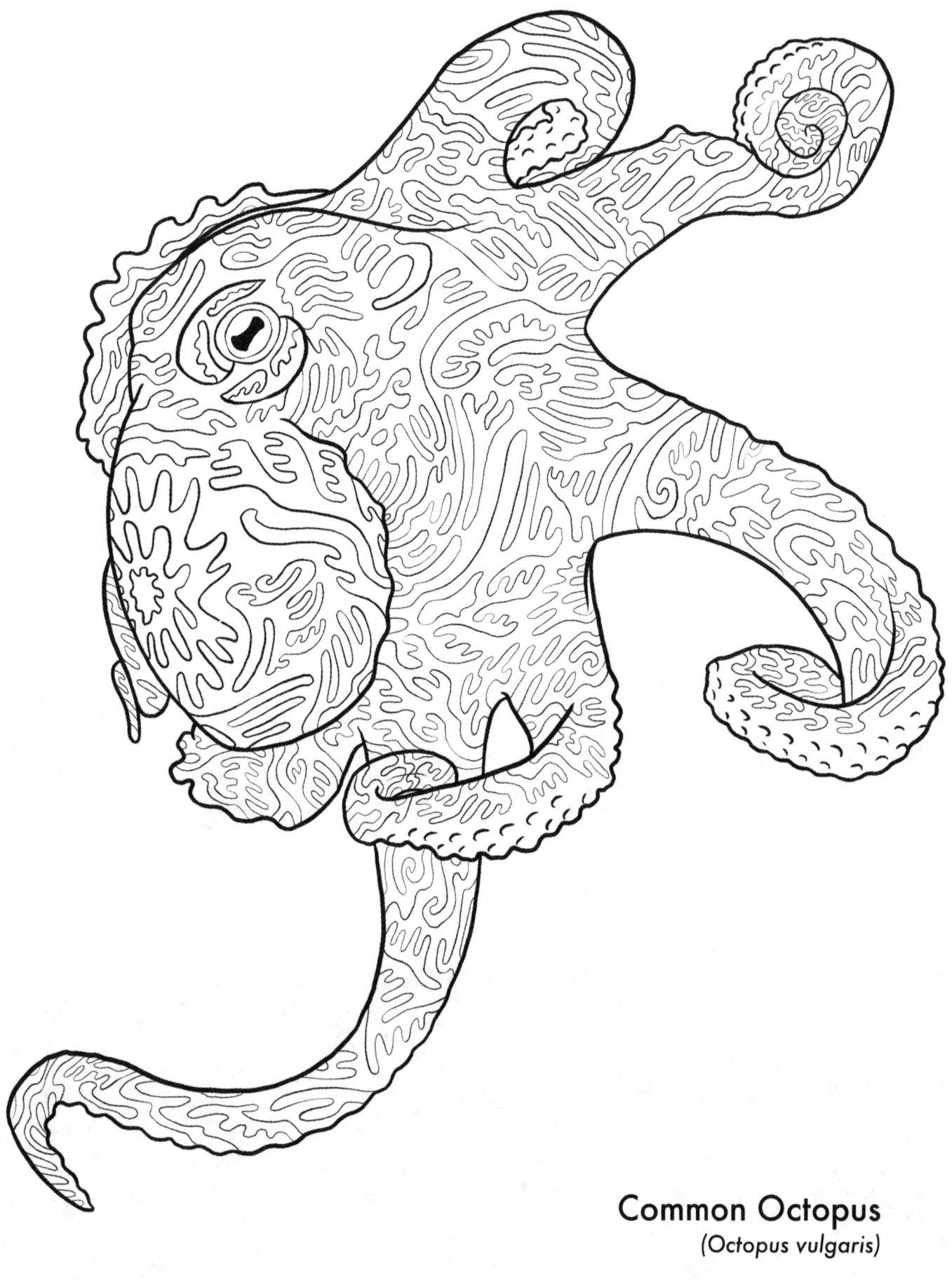

Common Octopus
(Octopus vulgaris)

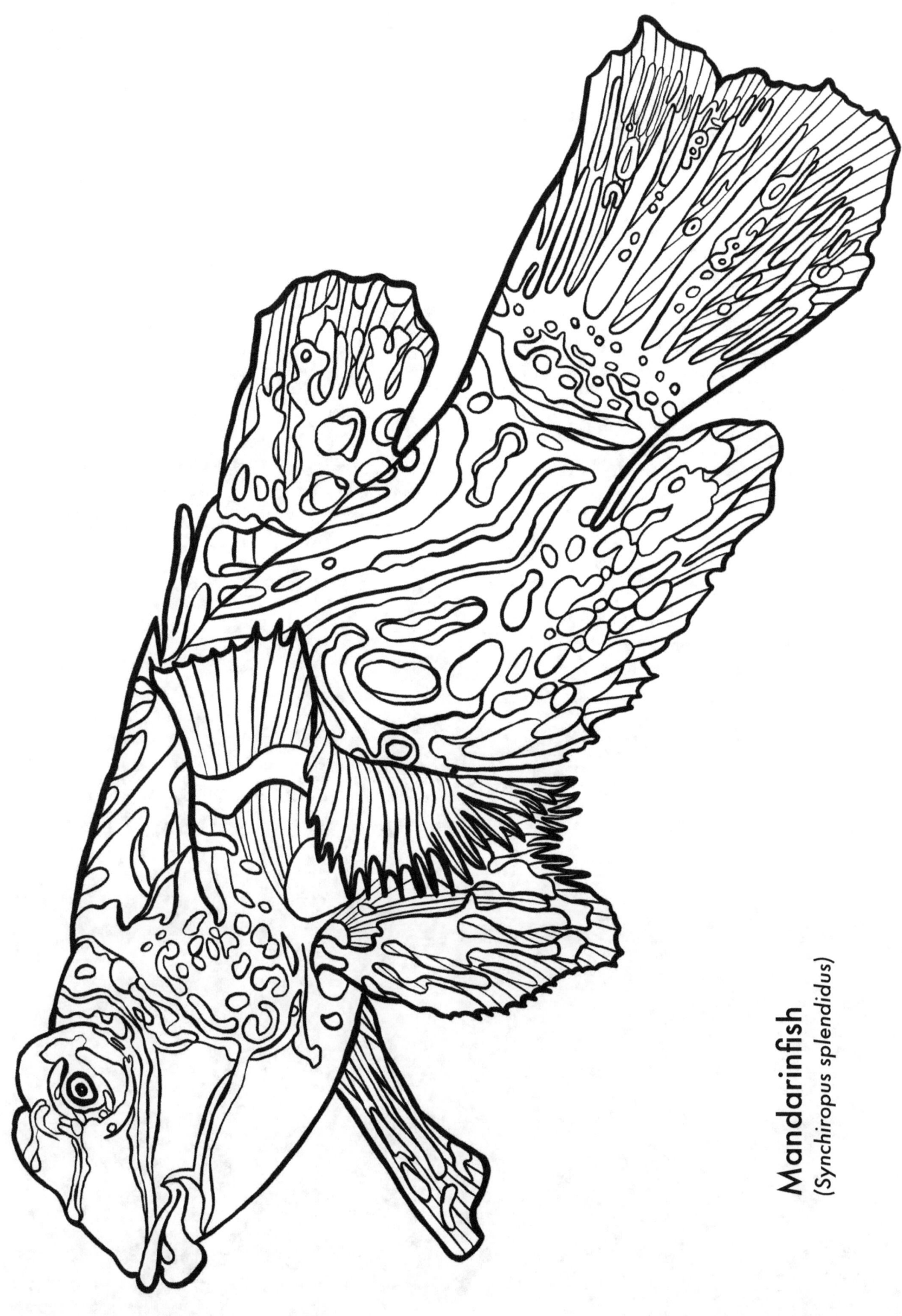

Mandarinfish
(*Synchiropus splendidus*)

Purple-Striped Jelly (Chrysaora colorata)

Commonly found in California's Monterey Bay, the Purple-Striped Jelly subsists on zooplankton and other small sea creatures. Around 70 cm in length, they have a white semi-translucent coloring with purple stripes on the bell. When touched, one of their eight marginal tentacles discharges a paralyzing sting to the prey, which then bends in to the four oral arms. These are used to transport the food in to their gastrovascular cavity. Though the sting is painful for humans, leatherback turtles have evolved defenses against this jelly and are considered their main predator.

Bluelined Angelfish (Chaetodontoplus septentrionalis)

The Bluelined Angelfish lives in the Western Pacific reefs, from the Northern reaches of the Malay Peninsula to the waters of southern Japan. Like other marine angelfish, they subsist on weeds and benthic algae, as well as zoobenthos like sponges and sea squirts. Adults live alone or in pairs, and very rarely have been seen in groups of three. From juvenile to adulthood, these fish can range in size from 4 to 25 cm.

Common Cuttlefish (Sepia officinalis)

Also called the European Common Cuttlefish, this species is found in the Mediterranean Sea as well as the Baltic and North Seas. During the day, they bury themselves in sand or mud, hunting at night for shrimp, crabs, small fish and molluscs, and in desperate times, even other cuttlefish. These are the largest species of cuttlefish, with a mantle length (not including head and arms) of up to 50 cm and a weight of 4 kg. Though they have many predators, such as dolphins, seals, and sharks, the cuttlefish is equipped with many defenses. These include expelling ink to distract and disorient the predator, and camouflaging abilities which allow them to change both their skin's color and texture.

Common Octopus (Octopus vulgaris)

The Common Octopus is a global species, with a range encompassing most of the Atlantic Ocean and the Mediterranean Sea. While the mantle grows to 25 cm in length, the arms can be up to 1 metre long. While they eat almost anything in their path, crabs, crayfish, and bivalve molluscs are their preferred meals. The meal is drawn inside to the beak, which is used to crack the hard shells to reach the meat inside. The octopus has three hearts, one main two-chambered heart supported by smaller branchial hears next to their gills. Like the cuttlefish, it can change color and texture to blend in with its environment.

Mandarinfish (Synchiropus splendidus)

The Mandarinfish is a small, brightly colored dragonet, only about 6 cm in size. they can be found in the Western Pacific, all the way from Japan's Ryukyu Islands to Australia. Within this range they are reef dwellers, bottom-feeders which feed continuously through the day and subsist on small crustaceans, fish eggs, and worms. As a defense mechanism against any potential predators, mandarinfish are equipped with tiny spines which secrete a toxin-filled mucous. Their bodies are coated in this mucous, which also emits a foul stench as an extra deterrent.

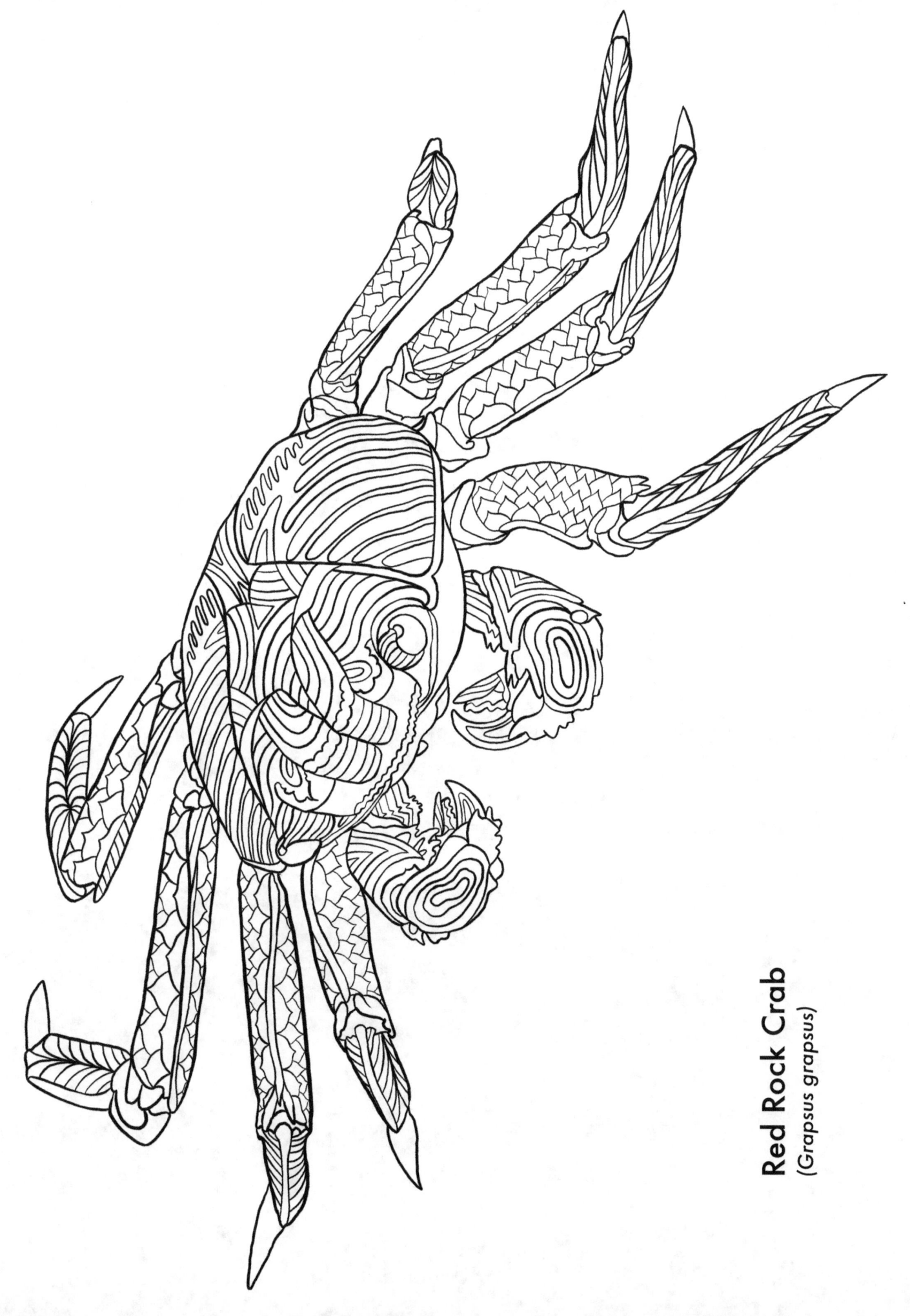

Red Rock Crab
(*Grapsus grapsus*)

Tiger Snout Seahorse
(Hippocampus subelongatus)

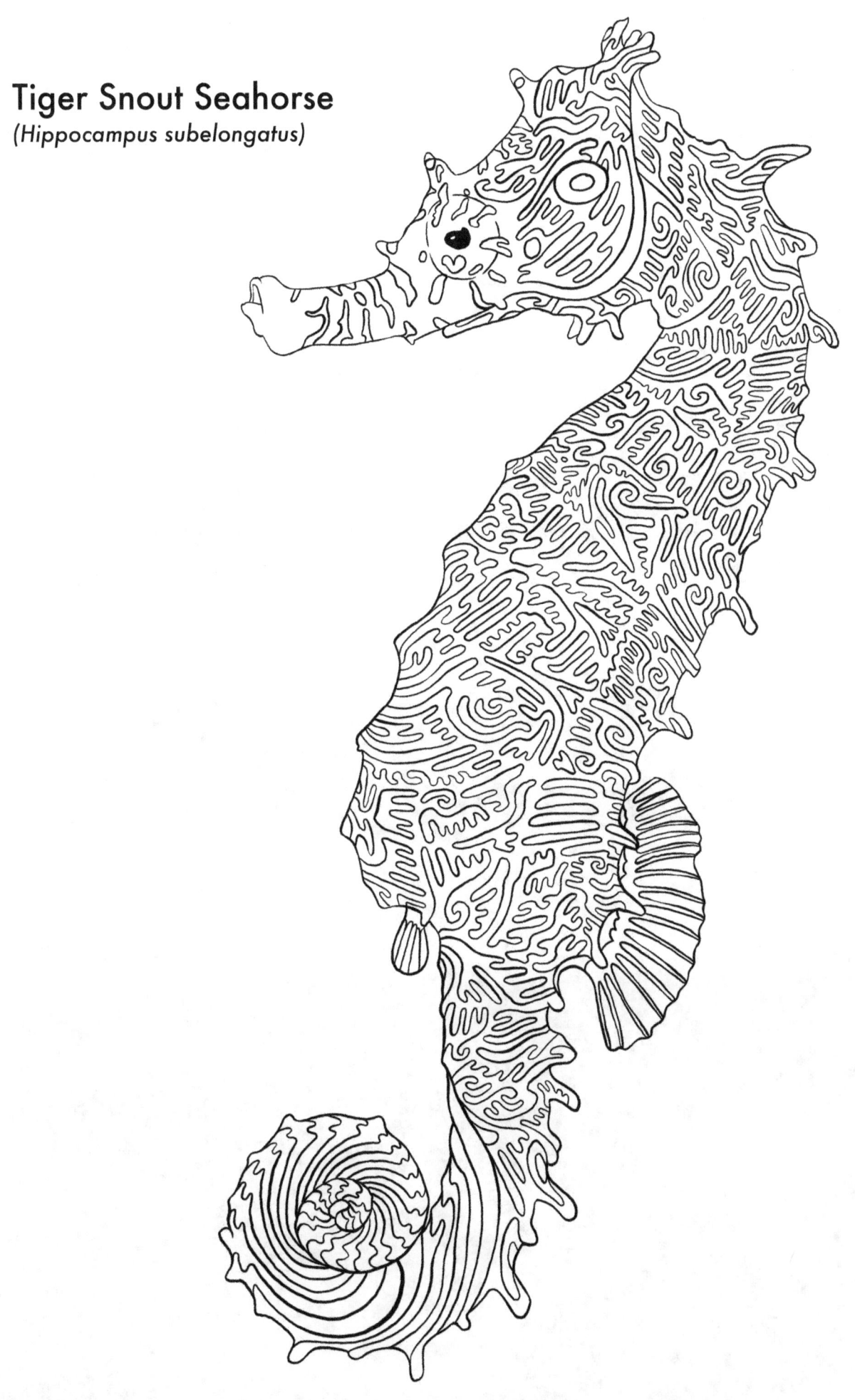

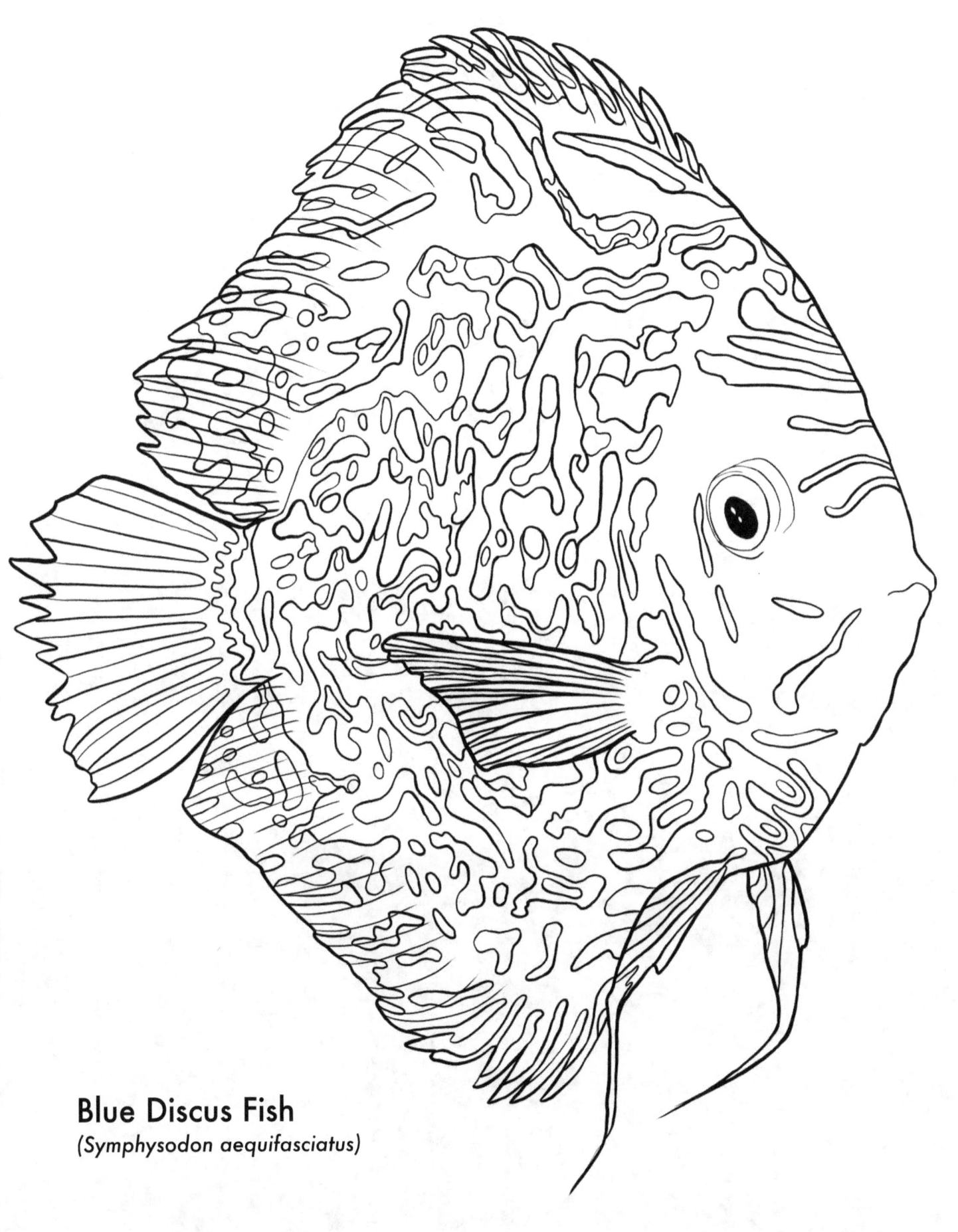

Blue Discus Fish
(Symphysodon aequifasciatus)

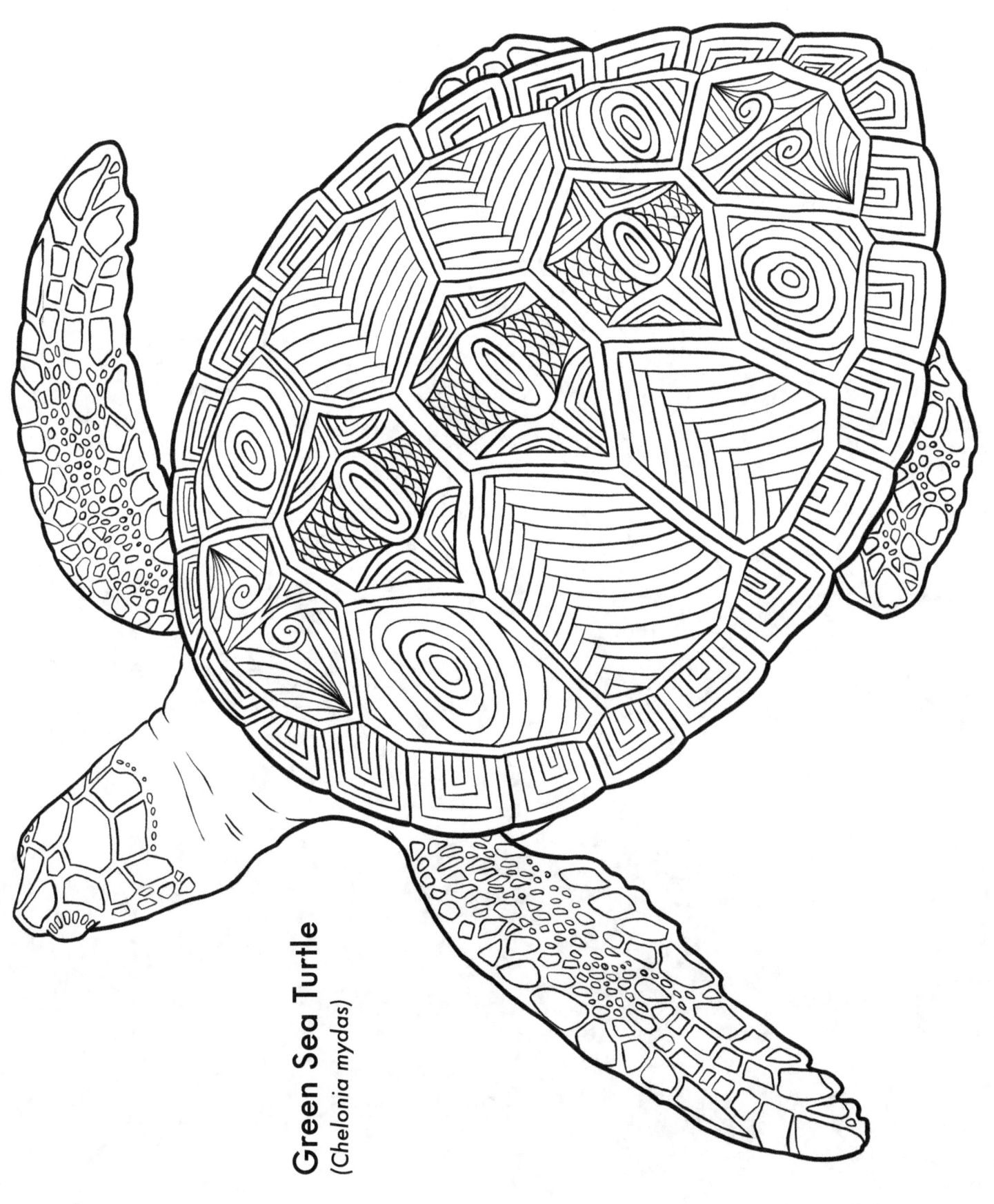

Green Sea Turtle
(Chelonia mydas)

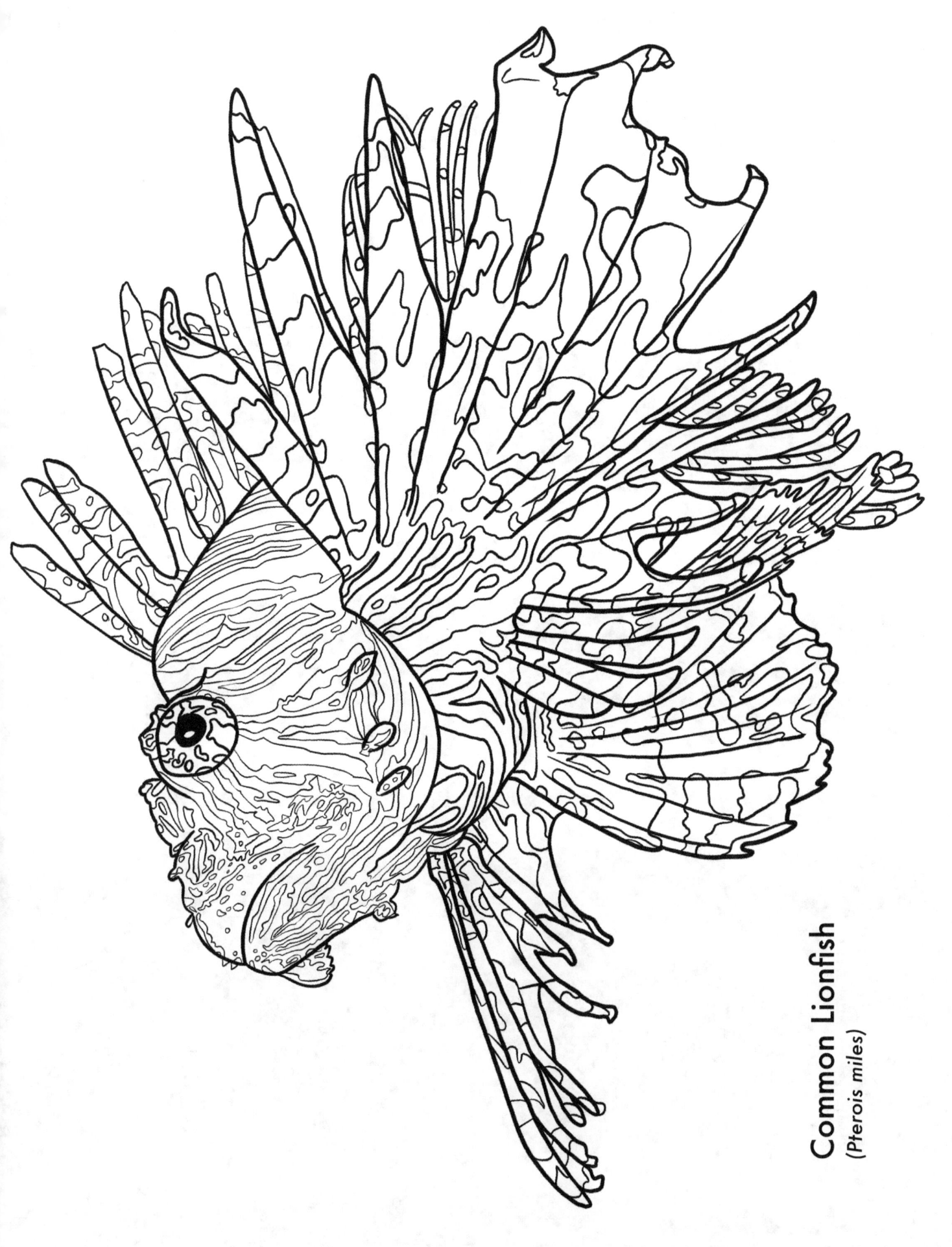

Common Lionfish
(Pterois miles)

Red Rock Crab (Grapsus grapsus)

Grapsus grapsus, also known as Abuete Negro, is one of three crab species along the Americas western coast known as the Red Rock Crab. This particular species is found from Mexico to Northern Peru, as well as in the Galápagos Islands. The carapace measures just over 8 cm. Like other crab species, it feeds on algae and sometimes dead animals. On the Galápagos, the abuete negro has been seen partaking in a symbiotic relationship with marine iguanas, cleaning ticks and other parasites from the skin to eat.

Tiger Snout Seahorse (Hippocampus subelongatus)

The Tiger Snout or West Australian Seahorse is found in the waters of south-western Australia, in rocky areas and muddy sea-bottoms with murky water. As adults, they range in height from 13 to 20 cm. these seahorses are monogamous, and the female lays her eggs in the male's brood pouch. During early summer, these seahorses move to the mouth of the Swan River, providing food for their offspring. They feed diurnally on small crustaceans and zooplankton which inhabit the waters.

Blue Discus Fish (Symphysodon aequifasciatus)

The Blue Discus Fish is found in the central and eastern rivers of the Amazon Basin, preferring floodplains and flooded forests. They range in size from 12 to 15 cm, weighing 150 to 250 grams. Discus fish feed on algae and small invertebrates, though the carnivorous make-up of this diet varies with low and high-water seasons. As highly social fish, these animals live in large groups, though breeding pairs move away when taking care of their young. Rare in fish, these species feed their larvae with secretions from their skin during the first four weeks of life.

Green Sea Turtle (Chelonia mydas)

UP to 1.5 metres long and 190 kg in weight, the Green Sea Turtle is found in the tropical and subtropical waters of both the Atlantic and Pacific Oceans. They are a migratory animals, travelling up to 2,600 km between nesting and feeding grounds. Mature turtles return to the sandy beaches where they hatched to lay their own eggs. Eggs are laid in holes and covered in sand, after which the female turtle returns to the ocean. After 50 to 70 days, the hatchlings emerge together at night, heading to the ocean themselves. Many don't survive, preyed upon by gulls and crabs. As juveniles, the turtles subsist on a variety of other sea creatures including jellyfish, sponges, and crustaceans, but as they mature they begin eating algae and sea grass as well. As adults, the habitat includes inshore lagoons and coral reefs, with juveniles living in the open ocean.

Common Lionfish (Pterois miles)

The Common Lionfish is native to Indo-Pacific waters, from East Africa to Indonesia. It has also been found in the Caribbean Sea as an invasive species. They are nocturnal hunters, feeding on small crustaceans and various fish which sometimes include smaller lionfish. They can grow to 35 cm in length. During the day lionfish hide in crevices within the coral reefs where they live. This creature is covered in highly venomous spines which have been known to kill humans. While they have few predators, the bluespotted cornetfish, moray eels, groupers, and reef sharks have been known to hunt the lionfish.

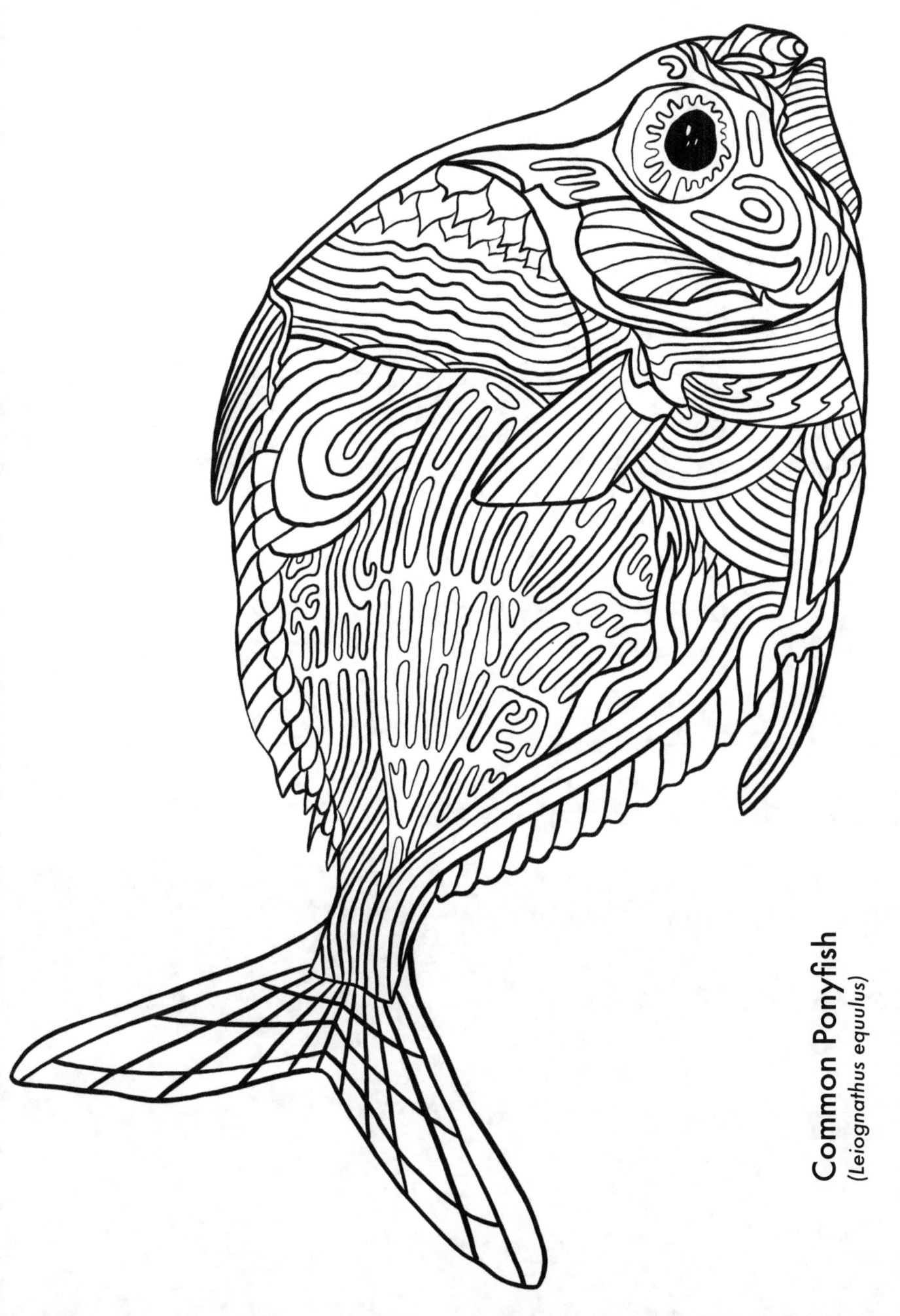

Common Ponyfish
(*Leiognathus equulus*)

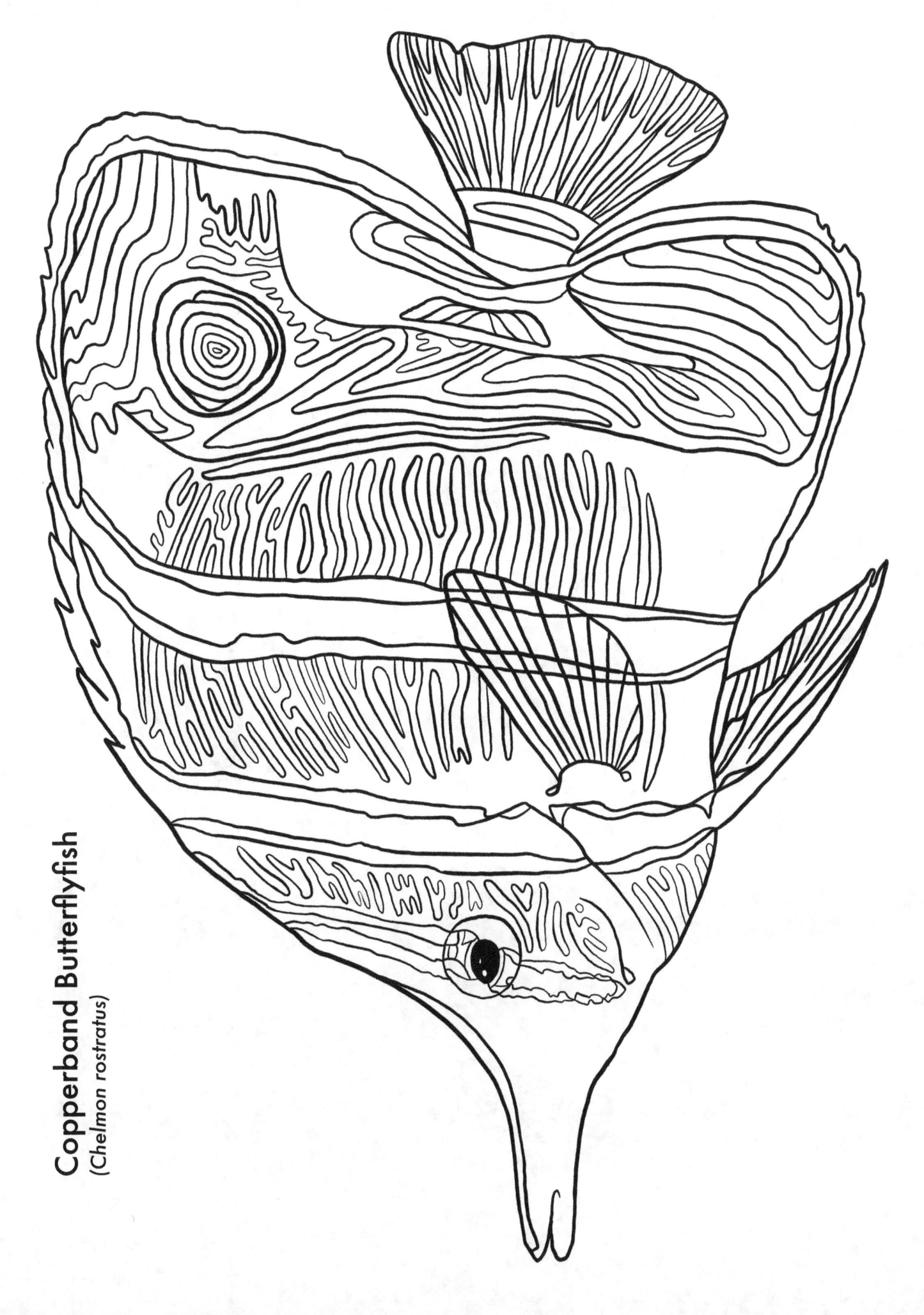

Copperband Butterflyfish
(*Chelmon rostratus*)

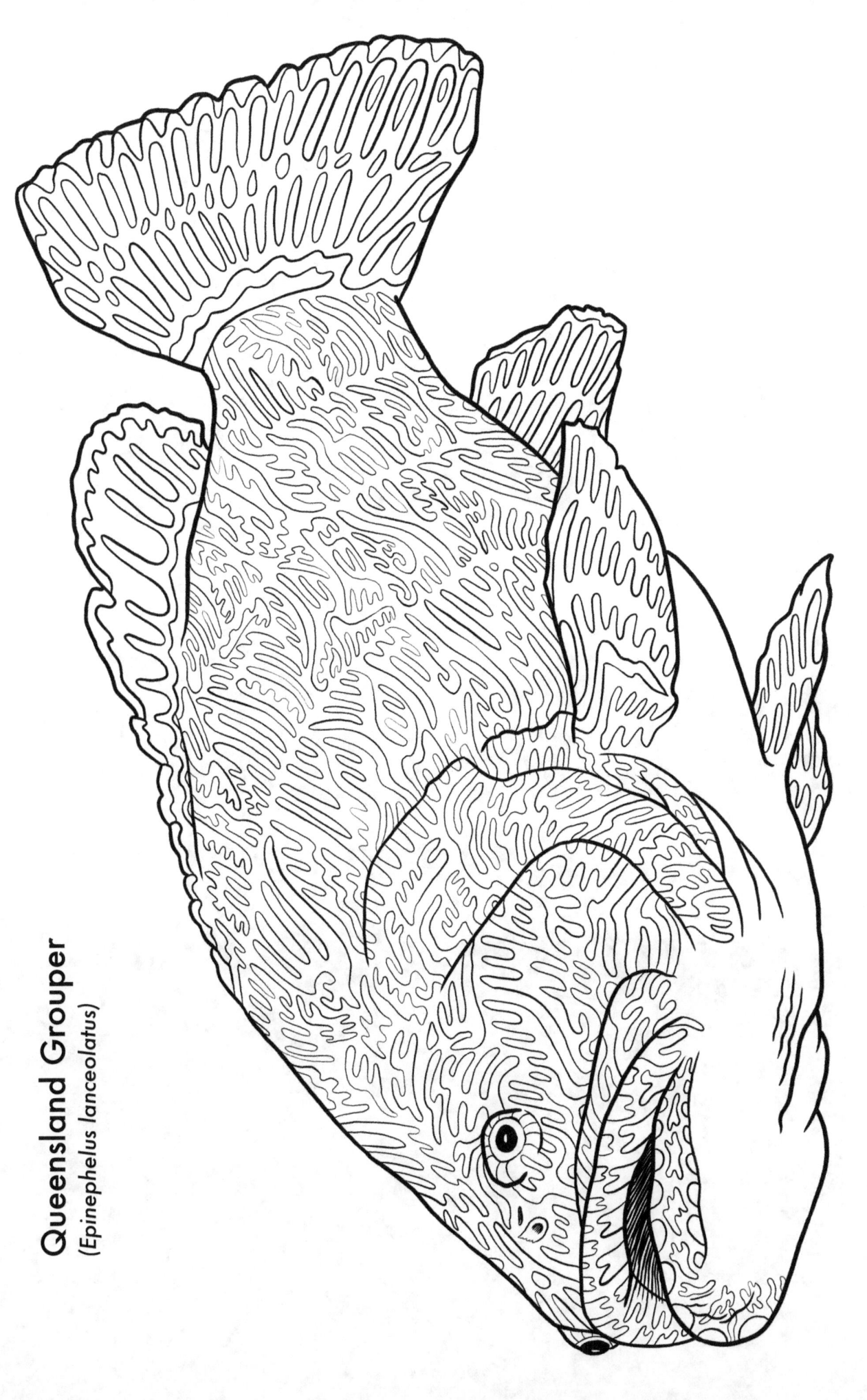

Queensland Grouper
(*Epinephelus lanceolatus*)

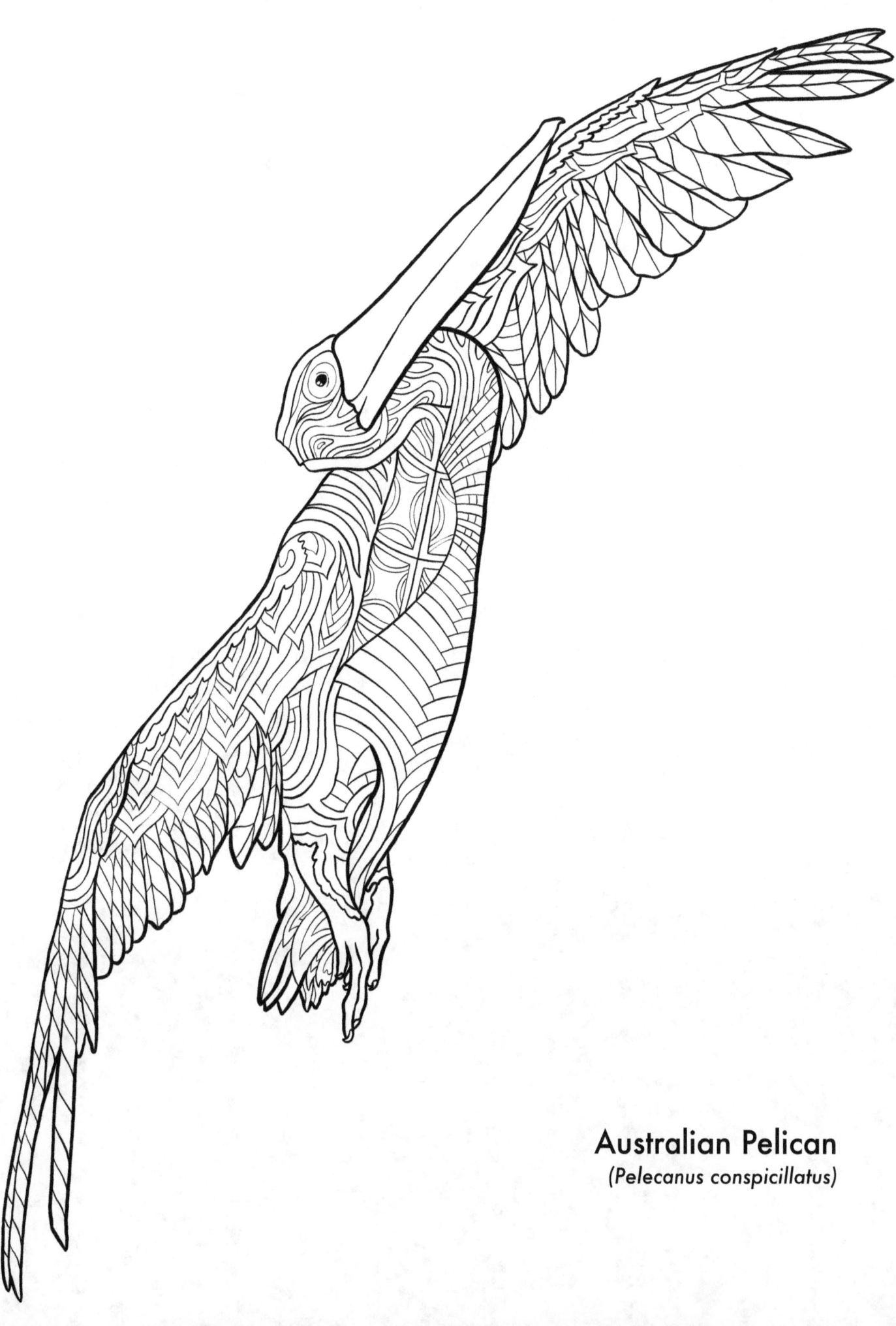

Australian Pelican
(*Pelecanus conspicillatus*)

Sperm Whale
(Physeter macrocephalus)

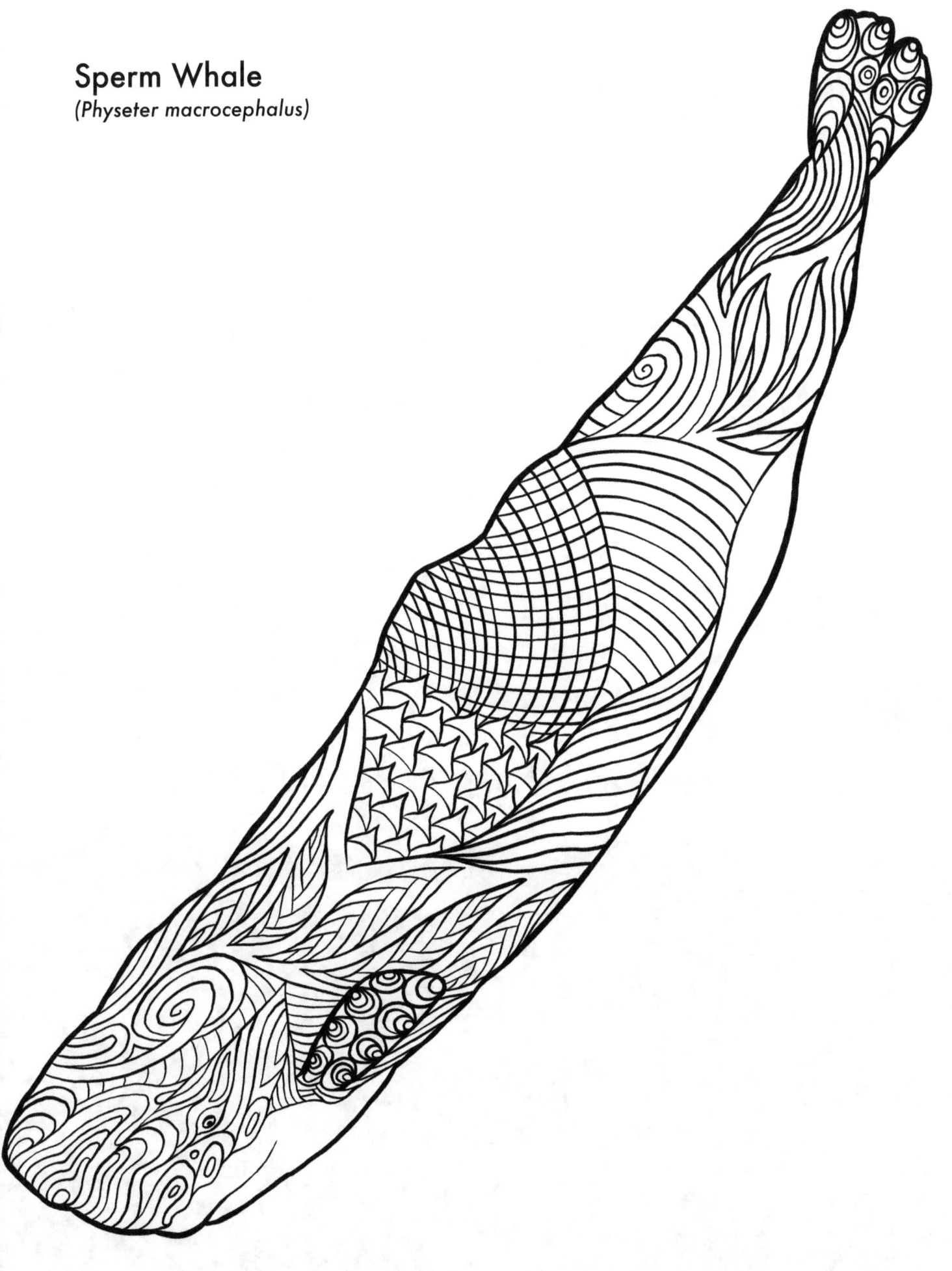

Common Ponyfish (Leignathus equulus)

The Common Ponyfish is found from East Africa to Fiji, as well as in the Red Sea and Persian Gulf. Intriguingly, they possess a light-producing organ in their throats which holds a bioluminescent bacteria to project light on their bellies. One of the proposed uses for this symbiotic relationship is as a form of camouflage, to blend in from below with the waters above. This fish can be found in muddy river mouths and the lower reaches of rivers. Common ponyfish can reach 30 cm in length. Traveling in schools, they feed on bristleworms, small crustaceans, and other small fish.

Copperband Butterflyfish (Chelmon rostratus)

The Copperband Butterflyfish lives in the reefs of the Indian and Pacific Oceans. Growing up to 20 cm in length, this fish prefers the shallower waters of coral reefs and estuaries as juveniles. As adults, they swim out in the open in deeper waters near the sea bottom. They are a diurnal species and almost exclusively carnivorous. Their long snout is used to search out bottom-dwelling species from within crevices, which include small crabs, worms, and glass anemones to fill their diet. At night they sleep within sheltered areas on the surfaces of reefs.

Queensland Grouper (Epinephelus lanceolatus)

Also known as the Giant Grouper or Mottled-Brown Sea Bass, this fish has a wide-ranging distribution, from East Africa to Hawaii and southern Japan down to Australia. They can reach up to 2.7 metres in length, with a weight of 400 kg at its heaviest. Giant groupers are found in shallow waters, living in reefs and lagoons as well as underwater caves and wrecks. As ambush predators, these creatures subsist on crustaceans and fish, as well as juvenile sea turtles and small sharks. All are swallowed whole. They are protogynous hermaphrodites, meaning that they change sex at some point during their lifespan.

Australian Pelican (Pelecanus conspicillatus)

As its name suggests, the Australian Pelican is found on the inland and coastal waters of Australia, but also lives in Fiji, New Guinea, and Indonesia. their wingspan can range from 2.3 to 2.6 metres, and they weight between 4.5 and 7.7 kg. They have the largest known bill in the avian world, with the record measuring 50 cm long. The total length, including the bill, of most is 152 to 188 cm. they prefer open expanses of water to live on and search for feed, driving fish into the shallows before scooping them up in their bills. These animals also feed on insects and crustaceans, and sometimes other birds, from the eggs all the way to adults of certain species such as silver gulls and grey teal.

Sperm Whale (Physeter macrocephalus)

The Sperm whale is the largest toothed whale and toothed predator, averaging 16 metres in length with some growing to more than 20 metres. They dive down into the depths more than 2 km, using echolocation and vocalization to find their way. They are also the loudest animals in the world, with vocalizations reaching volumes of 230 decibels. They are found all over the world, though prefer ice-free waters. Their diet consists of fish and squid, including the giant and colossal squid species. Sperm whales live in social units, with matriarchal pods made up of females and calves while the bulls largely live alone, though sometimes for bachelor pods.

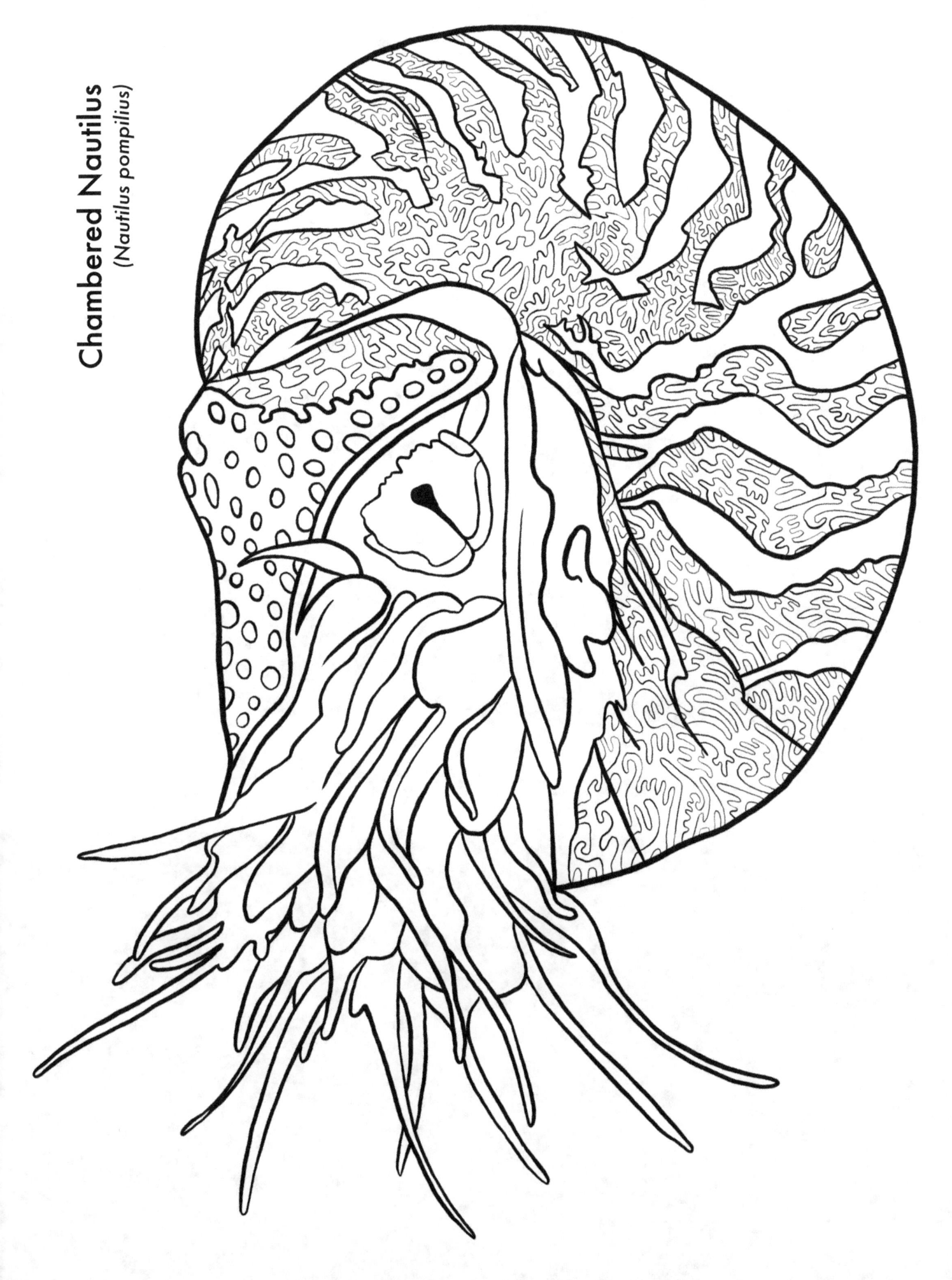

Chambered Nautilus
(Nautilus pompilius)

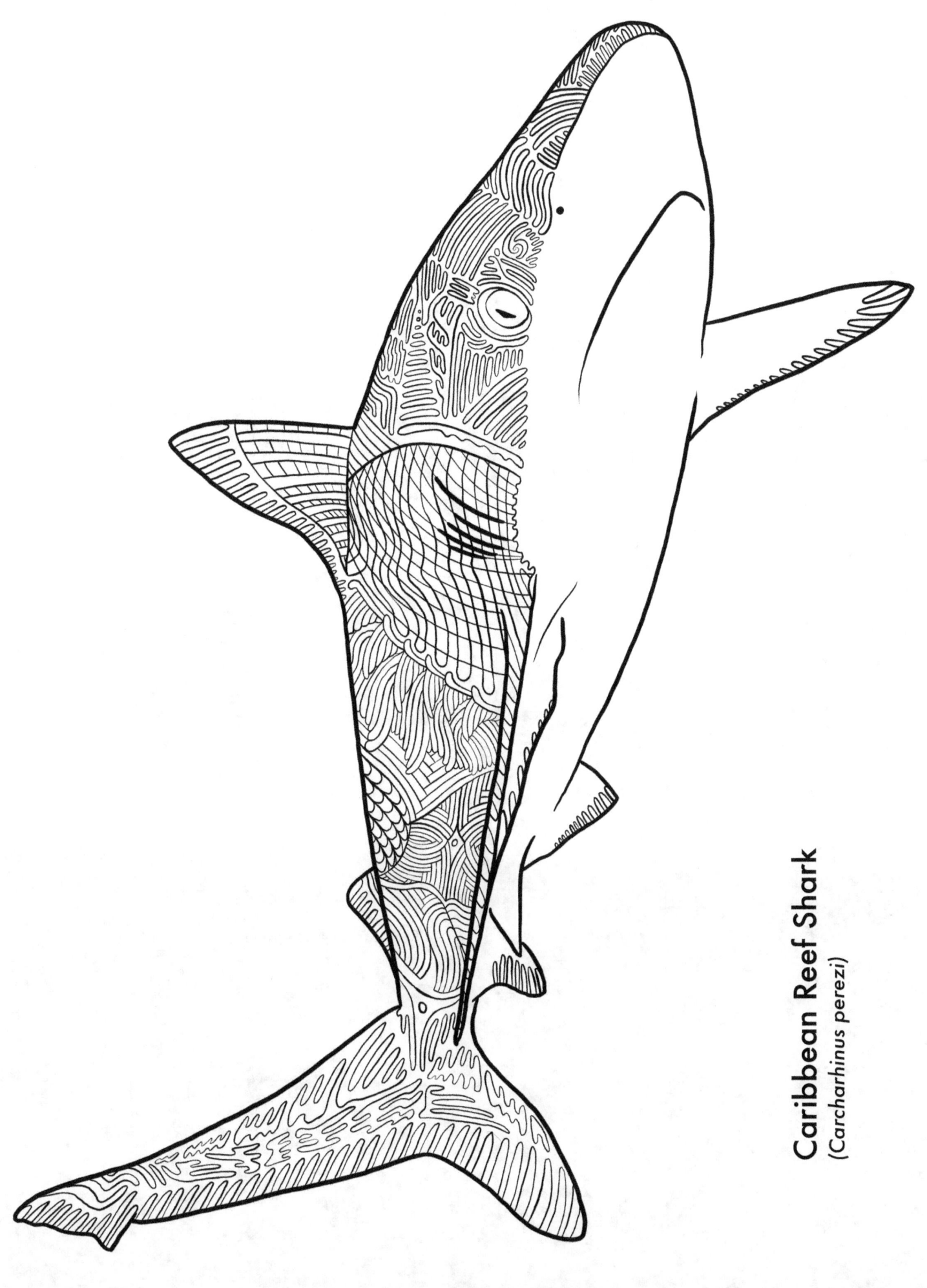

Caribbean Reef Shark
(Carcharhinus perezi)

Blue Crayfish

(Procambarus alleni)

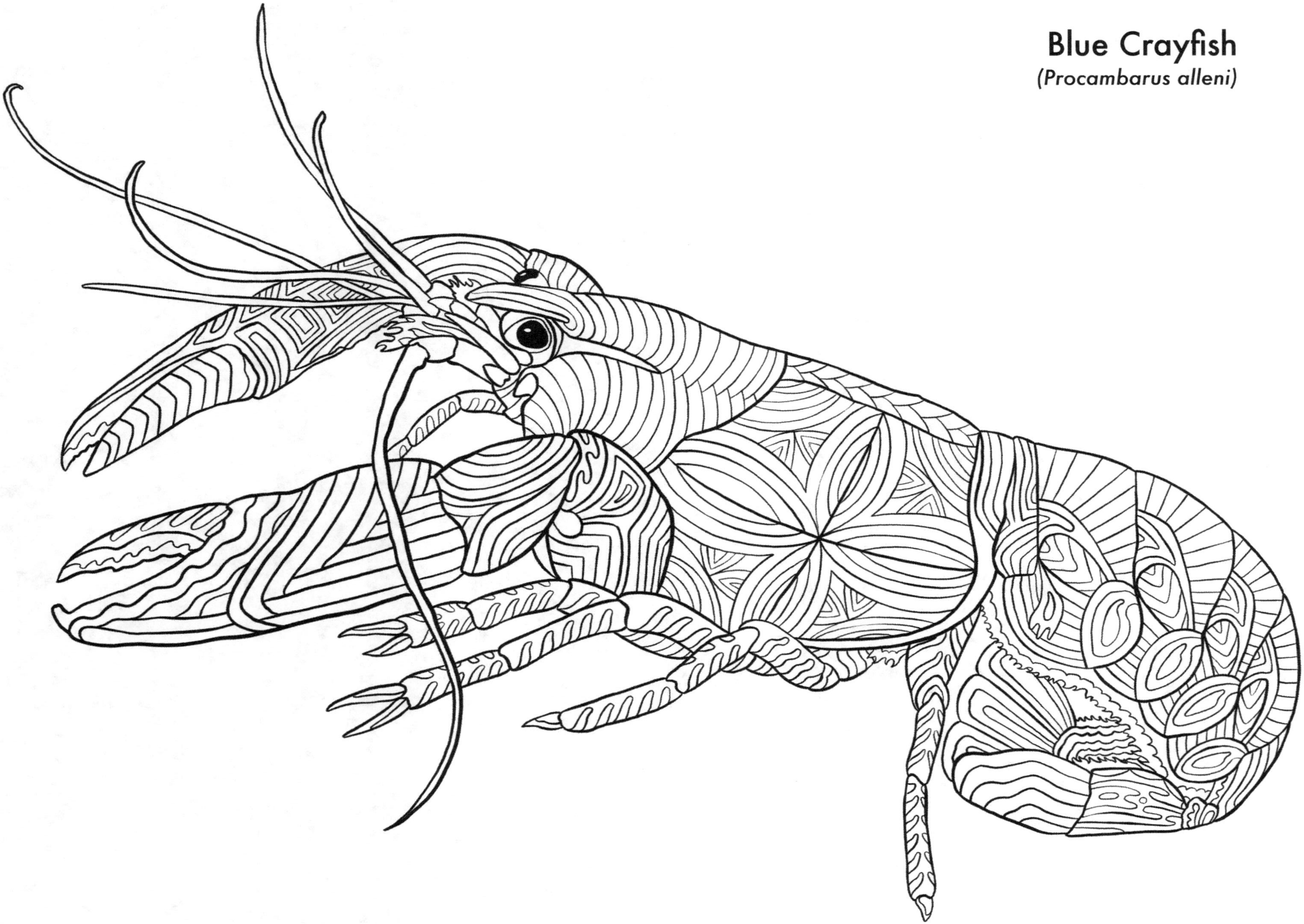

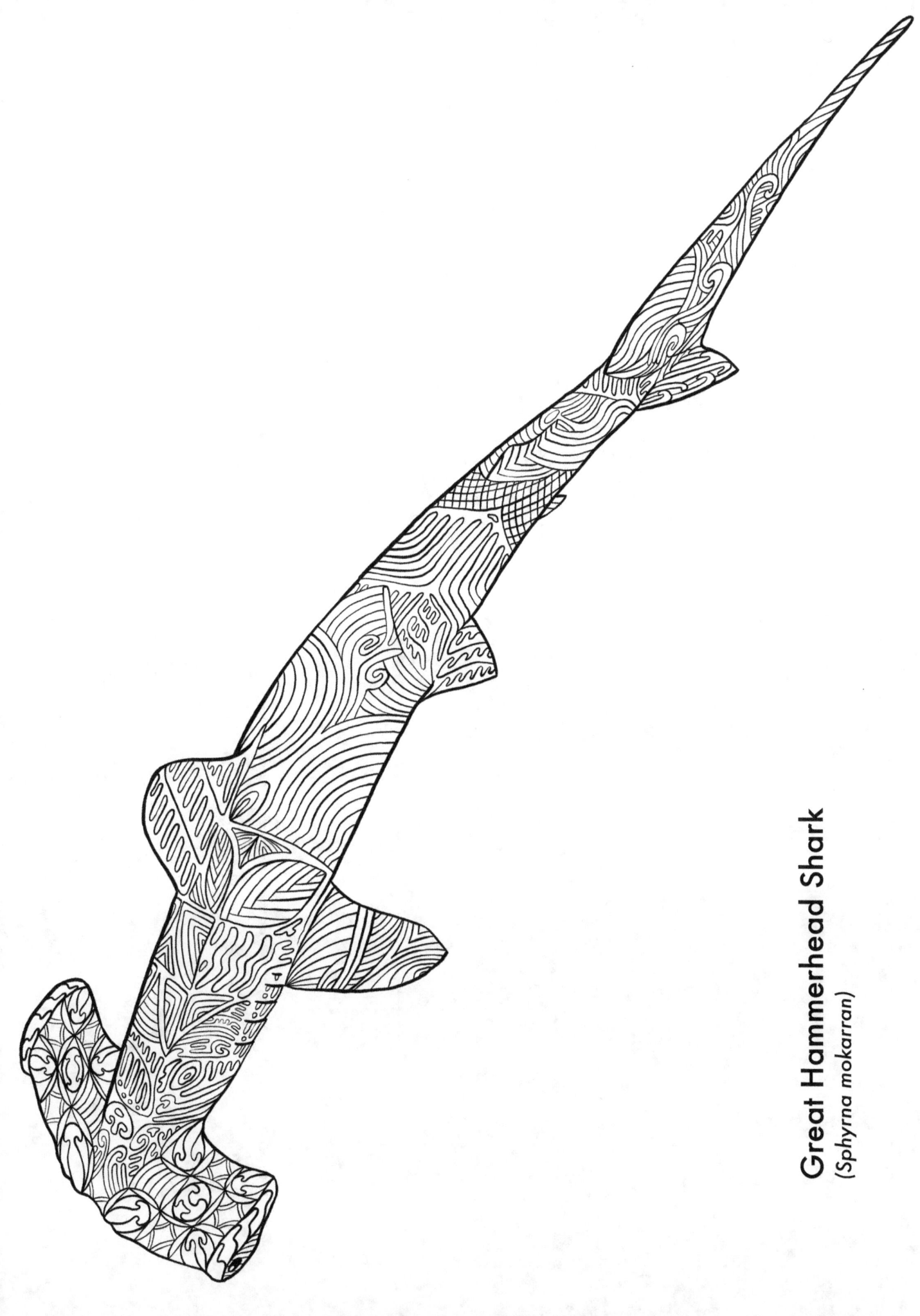

Great Hammerhead Shark
(*Sphyrna mokarran*)

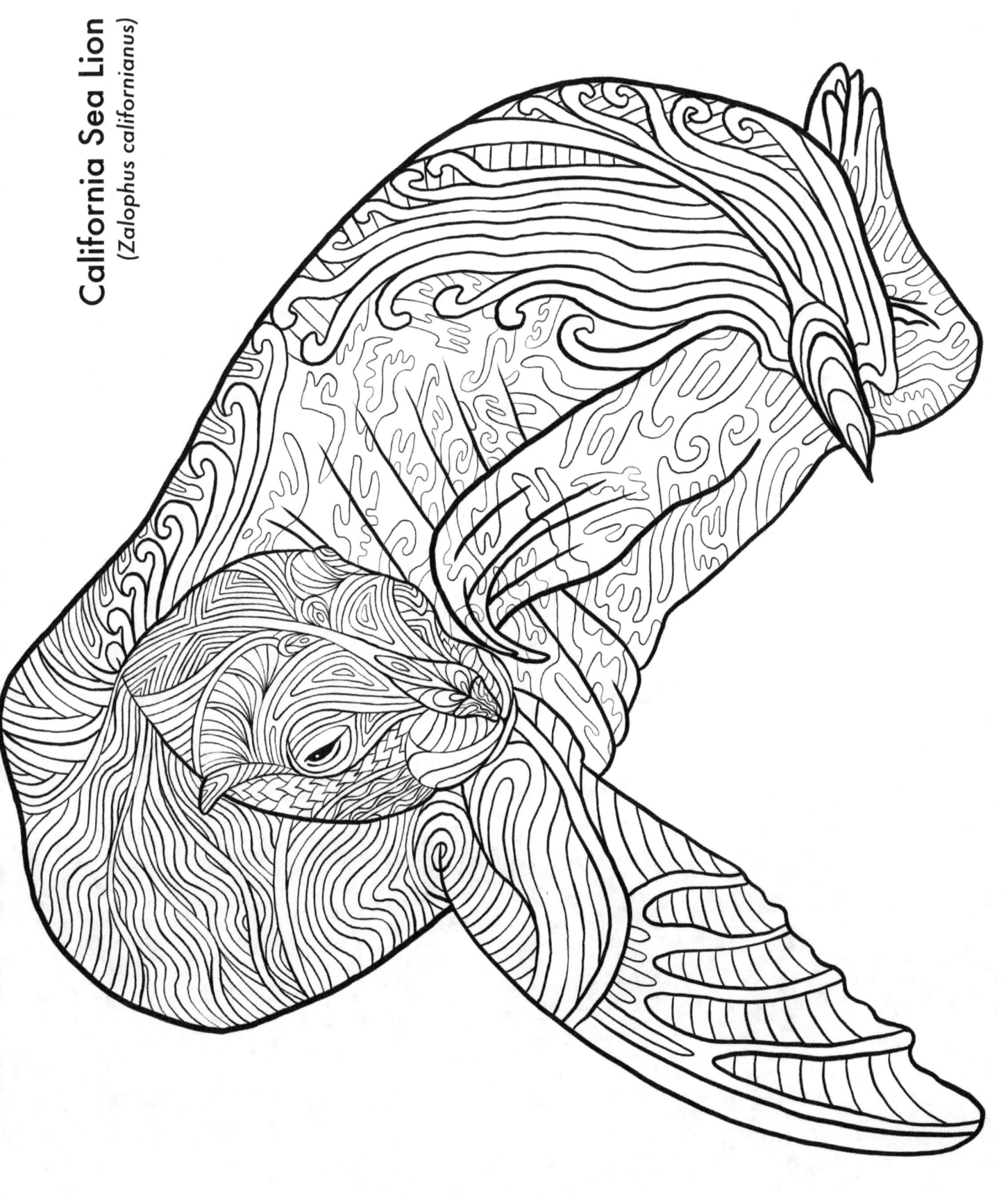

California Sea Lion
(Zalophus californianus)

Chambered Nautilus (Nautilus pompilius)

The Chambered Nautilus is found in the South Pacific, in both reefs and on the sea floor. While they are cephalopods, their tentacles do not have any suckers, and their eyes are far less developed than those of squid or octopus. To find food and navigate, these species have a pair of rhinophores near each eye, which are used to detect smells and chemicals in the water. They are mainly considered scavengers, eating both carrion and living shellfish. The shell is what allows the chambered nautilus to swim, filling and emptying with liquid to regulate their depth. They usually grow to 20 cm in length.

Caribbean Reef Shark (Carcharhinus perezi)

The Carribean Reef Shark is one of the largest predators in the reef, with some reaching 3 metres in length and up to 70 kg. They are found in the tropical waters of the western Atlantic, most commonly found in the Caribbean Sea. Mostly active at night, these sharks feed on bony fishes and cephalopods as adults, with younger sharks subsisting on smaller fish and crustaceans. These animals also seek out cleaning stations from time to time, where cleaner fish eat the parasites which gather on their skin.

Blue Crayfish (Procambarus alleni)

The Blue Crayfish is a freshwater crayfish found in mainland Florida, though it lives as well on some of the Florida Keys. They range in size from 10-15 cm. they feed on aquatic plants, algae, snails, fish, and rotting vegetation and animals which sometimes fall into the water. As relatively weak swimmers, they prefer to live in the rocks and the mud, and wait for food sources to sink down to them. These creatures are usually found in rivers and streams, as the currents prevent pollutants from gathering in their habitats.

Great Hammerhead Shark (Sphyrna mokarran)

The Great Hammerhead Shark lives in tropical and temperate all over the world, largely in coastal areas and the continental shelf. They measure from 3.5 metres up to 6 metres at the longest, with weights averaging between 230 and 580 kg. As migratory creatures, they travel from equatorial waters towards the poles in the summer. These solitary, nomadic predators, are found hunting at dawn and dusk. They have a wide-ranging carnivorous diet which includes crustaceans, cephalopods, as well as many different types of fish. The "hammer" is called a cephalofoil, and contains numerous electroreceptors which are used to locate the electrical signals of stingrays under the sand.

California Sea Lion (Zalophus californianus)

The California Sea Lion's habitat ranges from southeast Alaska all the way down to the coasts of central Mexico, and are often seen on sandy shores and rocky beaches, as well as marinas. As a sexually dimorphic species, males are generally 2.7 metres in length and weigh up to 350 kg, while females are around 2.1 metres and closer to 100 kg. they feed on a wide variety of mainly squid and fish, foraging and hunting near coastlines and on the continental shelf. Highly intelligent creatures, they have been known to cooperate with porpoises, dolphins and seabirds when hunting schools of fish.

If you loved this book as much as I loved creating it,
I'd be grateful for your review so others can enjoy it as well.
Thanks!

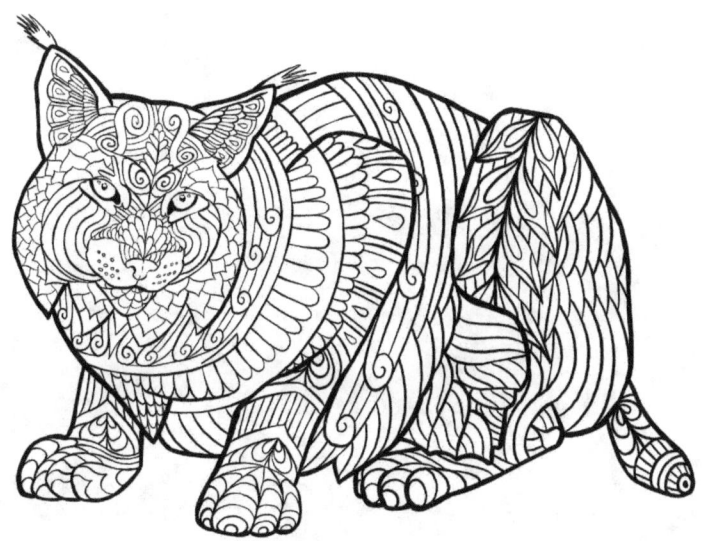

Check out my other adult coloring book:

Untamed Wilderness: A Wild Cats Coloring Book

And make sure to follow me on Amazon to get notified about new publications!